Jesus-Style Re[cruiting]

A Fresh Look at Recruiting and Forming Parish Volunteers

By Christopher Weber

VISUAL Dynamics Publishing

A Division of Visual Dynamics, Inc.

1216 Deerfield Point

Alpharetta, GA 30004

ISBN 978-0-9822997-4-6

©2011 by Visual Dynamics Publishing, a Division of Visual Dynamics, Inc. All rights reserved. No part of this publication may be reproduced, stored in a retrieval system, transmitted in any form of by any means, electronic, mechanical, photocopying, recording, or otherwise without the written permission of the copyright holder.

Biblical quotations are taken from the New Revised Standard Version of the Bible (New Oxford Annotated Bible), Oxford University Press, New York, 1991.

Acknowledgements

Many thanks to John Boucher, Director of the Office of Evangelization and Parish Development, Catholic Diocese of Trenton, and the parish leaders who attended two workshops that I presented for the diocese in late October 2010. His invitation and that visit caused me to shift the focus of the book from catechist to parish-wide recruitment. John and his wife Therese's remarkable work in evangelization also inspired me to heighten the emphasis on discipleship that you find in these pages. All of this resulted in a much better book.

The idea for Chapter 9 came from Fr. Keith Boisvert of St. Katharine Drexel Parish, Frederick, Maryland. Thank you, Fr. Keith, for allowing me to share your idea and adapt it to work with all parish volunteers.

You would not be reading this book if Joyce Crider, my editor and publisher, had not asked me to write it. I am deeply grateful for her persistence and long-suffering through all too many missed deadlines, and her expert help in bringing the book to life.

Dedication

For Laura, Ellen, and Eric,
whose patience and encouragement kept me writing in the wee hours,
and whose love makes God real in my life every day.

For my parents, Ken and Joanne,
whose unconditional love first showed me how to be a disciple,
and whose faith challenges me to keep listening for the call.

Contents

Introduction..4

Chapter 1 Level Your Program...7

Chapter 2 Warm Market, Cold Market..11

Chapter 3 An Old-fashioned Recruiting Method..15

Chapter 4 Go Face-to-Face...23

Chapter 5 Truth That Sells..29

Chapter 6 Discern the Gifts..35

Chapter 7 Initial Formation, Jesus-Style...43

Chapter 8 Less Thanks, More Constructive Praise..51

Chapter 9 Let Them Go..57

Chapter 10 Jesus-Style Recruiting and the Reign of God..............................63

Appendix..65

Introduction

Follow the example of the Master. Call first, train later, with the inspiration of the Holy Spirit! Implementing Jesus-Style Recruiting in your parish will keep you focused on making disciples, and will supercharge adult formation.

"Come, follow me."

We have marveled for centuries over those words of Jesus, and the gospel accounts of people instantly leaving everything to become his disciples. What happened in those recruiting encounters? Did they see something in Jesus' eyes, or hear something in his voice? Did they really leave their old life and livelihood behind? Did they follow him unreservedly? And what inspired Jesus to choose the people he chose?

"Come, follow me."

These same disciples walk with Jesus. They listen to his teachings about the Kingdom. They watch him heal and cast out demons, and then give it a try themselves when they are sent out on mission. They note the authoritative way he talks about his heavenly Father. They hear his warnings about the sufferings to come. They dole out miraculous amounts of loaves and fishes. They learn who is the greatest, how to love, and what it means to be poor in spirit.

"Come, follow me."

Just a few short years later, these same disciples abandon Jesus. One betrays him. One denies he ever knew Jesus. The rest probably (we are not really sure) flee. In the time of Jesus' deepest peril and need, his chosen band disappears into the crowds. Why does it all go so wrong? Wasn't Jesus inspired in his choice of followers? If so, why do they lose heart so abruptly, so totally? His entire ministry of spreading the Reign of God hangs in the balance, as the lonely Son of God hangs from the Cross.

"Come, follow me."

Finally, the same motley bunch of disciples, minus Judas, bursts out of their sorrow and fear to boldly proclaim the Resurrected Christ. These courageous followers endure persecution and even martyrdom to spread the Word. The Church is born. The mission continues, and others heed the call.

What does this Gospel thumbnail suggest about how Jesus recruited people for ministry? And how might we follow his example? I do not think I have to go out too far onto a theological limb to make two simple assertions:

1. Jesus was a "warm body" recruiter.

Jesus didn't hand out a job description before recruiting disciples, and his would-be followers didn't take an aptitude test before setting out on the road. Much in keeping with the practice of itinerant rabbis of the day, he called them first, and then trained them later, as they walked and worked with him. The calling of disciples appears to be spontaneous and inspirational, rather than pre-planned and methodical. He certainly did not make an announcement for volunteers in the synagogue.

2. The people Jesus called were flawed and gifted.

Jesus did not recruit the most talented, affluent and capable people. His disciples not only learned by doing, but also by some disastrous missteps. Peter's denial and later redemption stand in stark contrast to Judas' betrayal, despair and subsequent suicide. There were no absolute guarantees that everyone Jesus called would respond in the way he hoped, but anyone who turned wholeheartedly back to him could find their way. Those who allowed themselves to receive the healing grace of the Risen Christ as he breathed the words "Peace be with you" would later accomplish amazing things in his name.

> **If Jesus recruited his disciples through inspiration, and formed them through on-the-job perspiration, then we are on safe ground to do the same.**

In the heyday of bumper stickers (the early '70s), my parents used to have one on their car that read, "Christians aren't perfect – just forgiven." To me that motto beautifully represents the saints and sinners who led the early Church.

It remains a great motto for our work today.

If Jesus recruited his disciples through inspiration, and formed them through on-the-job perspiration, then we are on safe ground to do the same. Of course, recruiting "warm bodies" in the 21st Century Church is going to require different tools than were employed in First Century Palestine! This book contains some modern recruiting ideas gleaned from common practices of network marketing, and other ideas that have just plain worked in parishes near and far. At the same time, it is grounded in the idea that finding disciples to spread the message of Jesus Christ is an imperfect science with imperfect people. It is, first and foremost, a work of the Holy Spirit. Staying firm in this truth will make our job as recruiters and formers of disciples much, much easier.

Jesus-Style Recruiting is Disciple-Making

Forming disciples of Christ is a task that most parishes take very seriously. However, I believe that most of us (myself included) lose this focus when we begin looking for volunteers. All too often we are more concerned with filling a hole in our ranks than helping a member of our congregation fulfill his or her destiny as a baptized Christian. If all you get from this book is helpful tips for building the ranks of your lay ministers, then I will have failed to communicate my deepest purpose.

While Christ started his missionary activity with a rag-tag band of warm bodies, he ended up with fearless, spirit-filled disciples, many of whom we would later revere as Apostles. I believe that we can start and end our recruiting process exactly as Jesus did: we can bring raw recruits off the street and lead them to deep and lasting faith, to performing incredible works in the name of the Lord. This work will be very challenging, but what good and fruitful work isn't?

Jesus-Style Recruiting is Adult Formation

For twenty years or more the Church has committed substantial resources to adult faith formation. We have named it as a priority, and put our money where our mouths were in hiring professionals to run adult programs. When times have gotten tough, and the inevitable financial belt-tightening has ensued, both diocesan offices and parishes have been compelled to cut back resources dedicated to adults. We find ourselves discouraged by how little progress we have made in adult formation over such a long period of time.

Take heart. Don't be discouraged! Read this book through the lens of adult formation, and you will notice how much adult formation you are already doing when you prepare anyone for ministry. Not only that, you will see in this process of Jesus-Style Recruiting an opportunity to extend adult faith formation to every member of your parish in a way that is both substantial and satisfying. You will also discover in this process wonderful tools for helping your parishioners to evangelize.

Wow. That is an ambitious agenda, isn't it? Read on to see if this book comes close to achieving it.

How to Use This Book

Even though all of the elements of this book are based upon practical insights that I have gleaned from parish and diocesan ministry, the complete method described here has not been implemented in any parish of which I am aware. Therefore, while I certainly want you to read the entire book, I encourage you to take the infamous "cafeteria" approach to what you implement. The chapters build on each other, and should satisfy the reader who likes to consume books cover-to-cover. However, I also wrote this book for readers like me, who prefer to move through the chapters more freely. Each chapter is self-contained, developing one major idea from beginning to end. Feel free to start by reading the Table of Contents and picking a chapter that sounds interesting

Another way to start would be to flip through the handouts and worksheets at the end of each chapter, and see what catches your attention. Finally, you can sift through the book by referring to the **Jesus-Style Recruiting Tips** at the beginning of each chapter. My hope is that you will troll through waste no time in finding stimulating and useful ideas that you can and immediately put to work any ideas that you find stimulating and useful. I don't know about you, but I get awfully tired of talking issues to death without ever getting around to the doing.

Chapter 1
Level Your Program

Jesus-Style Recruitment demands that you find a place for everyone. To do this break your volunteer jobs into levels: Providers, Helpers, Professional Career Volunteers, Semi-skilled Volunteers, Skilled Volunteers. Work with your parish staff to apply these levels to all parish ministries.

Hey, everybody has those types of days. You know, days when you just want to LEVEL your program: Take a hammer to your computer, shred all your records, and "fire" all your volunteers. You have had enough of cajoling, coddling, inspiring, amusing, tricking, or even using Catholic GUILT to get people to join you in ministry. You want to stop everything and start over from scratch, or…well…just stop everything. If you are reading this chapter hoping for that type of "leveling," you are out of luck. That's someone else's book. This chapter's "leveling" is about designing levels of involvement in your program, and providing a myriad of entry points into ministry.

> **Jesus-Style Recruitment Tip #1: Meet people where they are.**
> As Jesus was walking along, he saw a man called Matthew sitting at the tax booth; and he said to him, 'Follow me.' And he got up and followed him.
> Matthew 9:9

The idea is simple: Find something for everyone to do, by dividing all of your parish programs into smaller pieces and categorizing them according to commitment and skills required. The smaller the pieces the better, because you will need a lot of jobs in order to get everyone involved. The reason behind this idea is also simple: Jesus met people where they were. He walked along the sea to call Peter and others to fish for people (Mark 1.17); He called the tax collector Zacchaeus out of the sycamore tree so he could eat supper at his house (Luke 19:1ff); He even broke social convention by talking to the Samaritan woman at the well (John 4:7ff). We have to do the same – hold back our judgments and encourage people to join us with whatever contribution they can make, large or small.

Start by having all of your parish ministry leaders divide their ministry into levels. Multi-level ministry provides an entry point for everyone. In order to do it well, all of your various ministry leaders must work together rather than compete for volunteers. The broader the field of opportunities available, the more parishioners you will be likely to attract. Here is one way to divide the ministries, based upon the amount of commitment and training required:

Level 1 – Providers
These are people who do, make or prepare things for parish functions, often from the comfort of their homes. Time commitment is flexible and occasional, and attendance at parish events is optional. No training is required. *Examples: prayer intercessors, bakers of goods for program events, crafters, linen preparers, letter writers, senders of greeting cards, and donors of other goods.*

Level 2 - Helpers
This type of ministry is short-term and limited in scope. It requires little or no advance training, and minimal commitment beyond showing up. Recruits come right in off the street and go to work. Make sure that every program you plan has openings for a lot of these warm body recruits. *Examples: set up and cleanup crews, picnic helpers, greeters, office helpers, hall monitors, chaperones, car wash or fundraising volunteers*

Level 3 – Professional Career Volunteers
These volunteers have been professionally trained outside the parish, and can lend special skills to a parish event or ministry. Training required by the parish is minimal, but the time commitment varies with the task for which they are needed. Sometimes it is a challenge to match a person at this level with a parish job or ministry. Be creative! These volunteers can bring some unexpected excitement to your programs. *Examples: carpenters, professional cleaners, interior decorators, nurses, certified teachers, theologians, scientists, lawyers, engineers, architects*

> **Your most important lay ministers do not work for the parish.**

Level 4 - Semi-skilled Volunteers
This level of ministry requires orientation, some training and an occasional retreat or day or renewal. Volunteers may serve regularly, even weekly, but perform duties that do not require much preparation. *Examples: catechist aides, retreat chaperones, planning teams for key events.*

Pastoral leaders may disagree about which volunteers fall in this category. Use as your dividing line the amount of training needed to effectively perform the task. If the volunteer needs regular ongoing formation, then they will probably fall into:

Level 5 – Skilled Volunteers
These volunteers perform their ministry regularly, often weekly or more frequently. They require not just orientation, but significant ongoing training and formation. They regularly prepare for their service. They may be groomed to head their ministry, or eventually even become a parish staff member. *Examples: catechists, pastoral musicians, liturgy coordinators, retreat leaders, parish social ministers*

Engage, affirm, and support all five levels, as they are all very important to the life of your community. The first three levels will be particularly handy in the recruitment of "warm bodies." Recruits will be happy to share their time or skills in a limited, non threatening way. Use these levels as rewarding introductions into volunteer ministry.

Figure 1 illustrates how leveling can increase the number of people actively involved in your program. Most of the time, we recruit for the upper right quadrant, for volunteers who will be very committed and need a lot of training. Expectations for what these recruits should deliver are very high. Is it no wonder that when we finally get around to telling them the whole truth about their responsibilities they often run away?

Of course we can't stop recruiting for level 4 and 5 volunteers; they are critical to our mission. However, we will reach out to our entire parish community if we use the three lower levels of ministry to recruit as well. Get Mrs. Peabody to bake cookies twice a year for some of your functions. Next year get her to help set up a sacramental reception. Meet her where she is. My guess is that that half or more of our parishioners do not see themselves as having the skills to be Level 4 or 5 volunteers. In some cases this is simply not true, and we need to help them match up their innate talents with the tasks done by Semi-skilled and Skilled Volunteers. However, in many cases, they have perceived correctly. They do NOT have the skills to be, say, an RCIA catechist or a liturgy coordinator. Not only that, but they are not the slightest bit interested in obtaining those skills! If we limit our recruiting to Levels 4 and 5 alone, we will continue to have a very, very small core of Semi-skilled and Skilled Volunteers. However, if we provide opportunities for people to serve at Levels 1 through 3, we will have a much larger core of volunteers to draw on.

Figure 1.

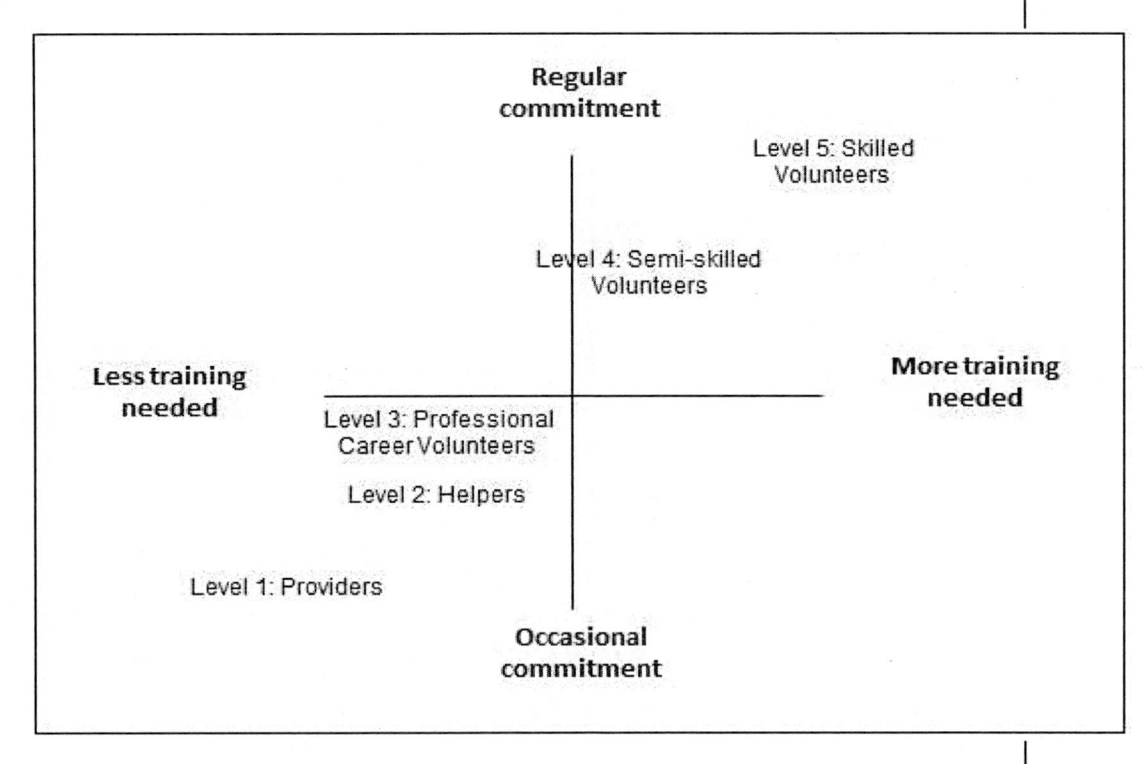

A chart with axes: vertical axis from "Regular commitment" (top) to "Occasional commitment" (bottom); horizontal axis from "Less training needed" (left) to "More training needed" (right).

- Level 5: Skilled Volunteers (upper right)
- Level 4: Semi-skilled Volunteers (upper middle)
- Level 3: Professional Career Volunteers (middle)
- Level 2: Helpers (lower middle)
- Level 1: Providers (lower left)

Here is **Challenge Number 1: Capitalize on Levels 1 through 3.** Find something for everyone to do, and make sure that the work is real work, and not "busy work." When I was a DRE in upstate New York many years ago, we held a very successful ministry fair that brought in new volunteers from all throughout the parish community. The event lost its momentum in subsequent years, not because of lack of volunteers, but because so many ministry leaders said to their new recruits, "Sorry, we don't need that type of help right now." Talk about a missed opportunity! We simply did not have enough jobs ready. I am convinced that if you provide such a variety of jobs, you will get an amazing and bountiful array of volunteers to do them.

Challenge Number 2: Stop fighting over volunteers. Most parishes do not have outright verbal sparring over volunteers, but we do often find ourselves getting the same people to do all manner of ministries. Develop your ministry lists for all levels in collaboration with other leaders in the parish. Note the ways in which Level 1, 2 and 3 volunteers can be incorporated across many different ministry areas, and plan how to use them most effectively. For instance, "Stella" has expressed willingness to bake for you. You could have her provide dessert for the First Communion reception, or baked goods for the social justice ministry fundraiser. She could bake her famous brownies for the Christmas caroling party, and her heartwarming apple pie for the Women's Group. Plan wisely how you will use Stella across multiple ministries, and she will bake happily for years; ask her willy-nilly and without any rhyme or reason each time a need comes up, and you will burn Stella out before she gets to her third batch of brownies.

Challenge Number 3: Your most important lay ministers do not work for the parish. Over forty years ago, the Second Vatican Council reminded us in its Dogmatic Constitution on the Church, *Lumen Gentium*, that the special dignity of the layperson's ministry lies in what they do in the world:

> *But the laity, by their very vocation, seek the kingdom of God by engaging in temporal affairs and by ordering them according to the plan of God. They live in the world, that is, in each and in all of the secular professions and occupations. They live in the ordinary circumstances of family and social life, from which the very web of their existence is woven. They are called there by God that by exercising their proper function and led by the spirit of the Gospel they may work for the sanctification of the world from within as a leaven. In this way they may make Christ known to others, especially by the testimony of a life resplendent in faith, hope and charity.*
> (LG 31)

We get so caught up in parish work that we sometimes lose sight of our ultimate purpose. The reason you draw people into parish life is not just to get them to do something for the Church, but to strengthen them to live their faith in the world:

> *Upon all the laity, therefore, rests the noble duty of working to extend the divine plan of salvation to all men of each epoch and in every land.*
> (LG33)

Let all you do with lay ministers inspire them to be "light to the nations." This outward focus can go far to give your parish an authentic missionary spirit.

Chapter 2
Warm Market, Cold Market

Recruit across the entire spectrum of your parish market. Identify your Warm and Cold Markets, and strategies for getting Warm Bodies from each.

If you have properly "leveled" your program, you now have a huge array of ministries into which you can recruit. Many of you may find yourselves a huge step ahead of where you were before Jesus-Style recruiting. Just hold on, though; it gets better. We turn now from the actions of ministry to the people who do ministry in our parishes.

Think about the kinds of people Jesus called into ministry. We have already noted that he met people where they were. He also called them – ALL of them – to some sort of action. He called the self-righteous to repentance (Matthew 3:7-10); he called the poor in spirit to the joy of the Kingdom (Luke 6:20); he called the sick of mind, body, and heart to healing (Mark 5); he called everyone to care for one another (Matthew 25); he called all who believe to do the works that he did, and even greater works (John 14:12). He called, and he called, and he called.

Jesus was an equal-opportunity preacher. He bravely proclaimed the Good News to anyone, regardless of how they might react to the message. He was not afraid to bring the Word anywhere, and he often went where people least expected him to go. There is wisdom for us to follow in this straightforward stratagem. Like Jesus, we must waste no opportunity to share the Good News of ministry. Like Jesus, we must step beyond our comfort zones to find potential disciples in places where we hadn't even imagined they would be.

Jesus' wide-open approach to evangelization matches well with strategies used in the world of direct sales. Amidst fierce competition, a sales reps success depends upon his or her ability to constantly expand their list of contacts. They do so by finding warm bodies at every end of their market. We should do the same.

> **Jesus-Style Recruitment Tip #2: Bring the Good News to Everyone.**
>
> Jesus said, "Go therefore and make disciples of all nations, baptizing them in the name of the Father and of the Son and of the Holy Spirit..." Matthew 28:19

The "Warm" Market

For the salesperson, a "warm" market includes people immediately within his or her realm of influence. This may include family, friends, acquaintances or people with whom the salesperson has worked in another capacity. People working a business from their home often start out by making a list of 50 to 100 people with whom they feel comfortable sharing their product. Service-based businesses use mailing lists of previous clients, referrals from existing customers, or others who have used services offered by competitors. People in the "warm" market of ministry are "warm" because they are receptive to being recruited.

My first personal experience of the "warm" market was in 5th grade, on the playground. A girl came up to me and said, "Hey, Chris! Can you ask Jimmy if he likes Karla? She likes him." I wanted to say, "No, have Karla tell him herself!" but instead I complied, because I knew how hard it was to pass that information on directly. I didn't have any difficulty sharing the message with Jimmy. He was in my Warm Market – my friend.

In church circles, your Warm Market is often people who know you and like you. They are likely to respond positively to your recruitment requests. At the very least, they will be nice about refusing you. While church ministers often recruit from a large Warm Market, we do so only in a limited way. At the top of our list are highly visible parishioners who often come to us first, or respond after minimal prompting. This first wave of volunteers usually has a lot of energy and commitment, and can overcome monumental obstacles to get ministry started. However, this enthusiasm is difficult to sustain, and parishes often find their strongest people grow tired from being overactive and over involved. Find fresh recruits to ease the burden of these Faithful Few by pressing the boundaries of your comfort zone – your warm market.

> **WARM MARKET:**
> Potential volunteers who are receptive to the idea of volunteering...or at least open to person who is inviting them into ministry.

What sectors of the parish population are within your immediate sphere of influence? How can you expand that sphere of influence? Try a brainstorming session with all of the members of your pastoral staff, and perhaps even the pastoral council or leaders of multiple ministries. Charge everyone with developing a list of 100 "warm bodies" they could invite to ministry. Focus upon those who are readily available. Compare lists, and take special note of overlaps. Take special note if there is anyone in your group who would be better suited to invite a person on another list. Be sure to focus on "warm bodies," raw recruits whom you might be able to bring into ministry. Once you have a substantial list, consider which level of ministry might be appropriate for each person.

Some oft-overlooked groups to consider in your list of 100:

- **Envelope Users** – Check your listing of envelope users and regular contributors. Are any of them inactive in parish ministry?

- **New Families** – Do we invite ALL members of the household, from 9 to 90, to be involved in ministry?

- **Regular Church Goers** – Can you think of people who come week in and week out to Mass, but don't volunteer?

- **Entire households who attend together** - Might this be a signal that Church has special significance to them?

- **Seniors** – We do not capitalize upon the wisdom and experience of our elder members enough.

- **Grown Children who come with their Parents** – Note young adults who remain active churchgoers beyond Confirmation. They are here because they want to be here!

And who else? Who else might be ripe for ministry, yet overlooked?

Warm Market volunteers will be the easiest group to bring into ministry.

However, take note of one cohort that can pose a challenge. Many people on your Top 100 list may be there because they are already active in ministry! An active parishioner might feel that this is not the year to take on something new. If the recruits are interested in trying something modest, place them at a level that requires minimal commitment and training. Respect these volunteers, and don't burn them out. Be sure to coordinate your recruiting efforts with the person in charge of their current ministry.

The "Cold" Market

Once you get through the easy people to ask, you move into the hard work of recruiting. The "Cold" Market consists of people you don't know directly, and people with whom you have less contact. This is fruitful ground for recruiting nonetheless.

Here are some "Cold" Market Recruits:

- Couples/Families that show up for sacraments after years away from the Church.
- Registered parishioners who donate or attend infrequently.
- Inactive Spouses of Active Members.
- Extended Family Members of Parishioners.
- Public Figures who are known to be Catholic but have no parish.
- Registered parishioners who don't fully participate in the celebration of the Eucharist

Who else comes to mind? Is this a Cold Market or what?

It would be very easy to dismiss the people in this group. After all they are the players in just about all of the Worst Moments in Sports that we share with our peers. However, this is a good place to hold fast to the adage "a stranger is just a friend we haven't made yet." Who knows what might happen when we get to know these people? That is the principle behind two Cold Market strategies: 1) recruit recruiters and 2) evangelize.

To work your Cold Market you need to cast a large recruitment net. To do that, you need a lot of people fishing. By recruiting recruiters, you can transform portions of the Cold Market into a Warm Market. Let's say you ask your friend, Hal, to recruit for you. He is already one of your volunteers, and has totally grasped the ministry vision of your parish. You don't know Hal's friends and family members that well, even though they are parishioners. They are a Cold Market to you. However, they are Hal's Warm Market. They will be much more open to Hal's invitation than yours. Enlisting the help of a large network of recruiters like Hal brings your message to people who might not have paid attention otherwise. Your Cold Market begins to warm up.

COLD MARKET: Potential volunteers who are less receptive to the idea of volunteering...or indifferent to person who is inviting them into ministry.

Evangelize!

Once you have heated up as much of the Cold Market as possible, you will need to find other ways to reach out. To do this well, stay rooted in the idea that calling people into ministry is a way of sharing the Good News with them. Your work here is not just recruitment, but also evangelization. People you call to ministry will be better off when they respond. They will get to know Jesus, they will gain joy in living their faith, and they will feel good about livingly selflessly for others.

To get started, use contact list and referrals to identify parishioners who are at the periphery of the community. One great resource is your Parish Database. Work through your list of households to determine those who do not donate regularly, or whom you do not see regularly. Cross reference these parishioners with active churchgoers who live near them. Invite the active churchgoers to do two things:

      (1) take part in a Level 1 or Level 2 activity
      (2) invite their neighbors to participate in it with them.

For example, Sarah Jenkins, active parishioner, asks her neighbor, Wanda Field, to join her in making cookies for the youth ministry bake sale. They either drop off their food together, or one of them picks up the food from the other to take to the sale. Perhaps the active churchgoer invites the neighbor to bake cookies together, and during the baking shares friendly conversation with her neighbor about the church or the youth group. The Level Activity (Provider) becomes an occasion for friendly conversation, which may open the door to a deeper relationship with the church community.

Here's another way to evangelize: The last parish I belonged to offered a lot of sacramental recruitment moments. For Holy Thursday, the parish invites families of children who have received their First Eucharist since the previous Easter to lead the procession to the Altar of Repose at the end of the liturgy. They stand on either side of the hallway as people approach the Chapel. The parish also invites Confirmandi from the previous year to bear the Cross during Good Friday. These wonderful traditions invite families to greater participation in the Triduum. They draw people into the life of the Church. Other churches inspire households to service by having sacramental candidates write notes, host a reception or mentor a candidate the next year.

How will you reach out to people in your Cold Market? How will you motivate your active parishioners to build relationships with people beyond their comfort zone? This is not just a matter of good recruiting, but of healthy Church living. Recruiting within both our Warm and Cold Markets reminds us that everyone counts, that everyone is important in God's eyes. By involving people across the entire spectrum of our parish, we remain true to Jesus commandment to "love one another as I have loved you." (John 15:12)

While the Warm Market-Cold Market idea prescribes an effective method, take special care to remember that Jesus-Style Recruiting is first and foremost about ministry. At one of the workshops I offered on this topic, a participant wondered aloud if it was a good idea to borrow recruiting methods from Madison Avenue. Another participant mused, "Nah, it's not a problem. I think Madison Avenue got their method from us first!"

Chapter 3

An Old-fashioned Recruiting Method

Engage your entire parish in the work of recruitment. Use this Gospel-based method to multiply your ministry

The whole town of Who-ville waits in the balance as the Mayor holds the youngest Who, Jo-Jo, over his head, and pleads, "Give a yipp! Give a yopp!" As the young lad finally gives a "yopp," the sound of the entire town yelling and making noise breaks through the atmosphere of their dust speck world. The dust speck is saved from being boiled in oil, and Horton, who first heard the Whos, is a hero.

This scene from the Dr. Seuss cartoon classic contains important wisdom for volunteer recruitment. It is not just a matter of "many hands make light work;" your work should focus on getting everyone in the parish working, doing SOMETHING, however small, to build up the Body of Christ. Here is a way to encourage significant portions of your community to give a "yipp" or "yopp."

Sell the Benefits

The very best business transactions happen when everyone wins; the salesperson sells the product, the buyers are content with the price, and all find, to their complete satisfaction, that the product is the ideal solution for their needs. Consumers tell others about the product, and the salesperson gets more and more customers. When recruiting volunteers, you must set this "win-win" scenario as your goal. From the outset, fix in your mind that your volunteers have the most to gain by giving generously of their time.

Believe the wisdom of Jesus: those who leave all for the Kingdom of God will get back much, much more than they give. Drill this idea into your mind. Say it forty thousand times to your volunteer. Say it until you believe it. It is true!

> **Jesus-Style Recruitment Tip #3: Share the rewards of the Kingdom.**
>
> And he said to them, "Truly I tell you, there is no one who has left house or wife or brothers or parents or children, for the sake of the kingdom of God, who will not get back very much more in this age, and in the age to come eternal life." - Luke 18:29-30

It is time to come clean. How many times have you started a recruitment talk with a potential volunteer (let's call her Maria) like this?

"Maria, I know you are really, really busy this time of year. And I know you have a lot of activities going on with the kids in school. And I know you have a lot on your plate with your father-in-law in the hospital, your new responsibilities in the Quilt Makers' Guild, and that you are working very hard to single-handedly remodel your home...BUT..."

This "I-hate-to-ask-you" lead-in is deadly. It implies that what you are about to ask

the person to do is barely worth consideration. If you really hate to ask people to join you in the enterprise of Spreading the Good News, then it must be a pretty annoying and unsatisfying work. Believe in the fantastic benefits of teaching the Gospel of Jesus Christ with others, and share this as the best thing that could possibly happen to them.

Reconnect with your zeal for the Gospel. Search deeply for it. Don't recruit a single person for ministry unless you are convinced of the gift. Then, set them on fire with the zeal, too! Your conviction is an integral part of the contagion. If you feel that you have to apologize for asking others to help, then you don't have it yet. Go to prayer, and ask God to relight your fire. Once you rediscover your zeal, you can begin "selling" the message to others. It will be easy to ask them to join you, because you will know, deep down, that you are offering them not a burden, but an incredible gift. With your faith fire lit to a fierce blaze, you can begin recruiting. However, don't jump right into recruiting volunteers. Take time to draw others into the ministry of recruiting first.

Step 1: Select One Ministry for Recruitment

Successfully implementing this step could be a revolutionary move for your parish. Gather decision-makers from across the parish to determine one ministry area for which you are going to recruit. Will you focus on evangelization ministries? Pastoral care? Liturgy? Catechesis? Look to your area of greatest need, or, if you have difficulty negotiating, select one at random. Working with just one ministry area per year will have a profound effect on that ministry. At the same time, it will prove helpful for the other ministries, because it will start your parishioners thinking systematically about how they volunteer.

There is no need to issue a "ban" on enlisting volunteers for other ministries; there will undoubtedly be urgent need to fill certain positions every year. At the same time, inform people across all venues of ministry that you will be zeroing in with a laser-like focus on the chosen service area. Encourage everyone to support this effort, knowing that their particular ministry will have its day as well.

Step 2: Parish Leaders Recruit the Core Team

Goal: 4 or 5 Core Team Members

In order to fully mobilize your volunteer force, find a small core of people who can invite others to recruit. In all likelihood, you already have these people in your ranks. These might be members of your pastoral council, some of your most seasoned and enthusiastic leaders in the ministry area, or just good friends who believe in what you are doing. The key here is to start with just four or five people whom you do not need to convince of the importance of the mission. This group of people will serve as your Core Team.

Invite this small group together for a meal, fun conversation, and then about an hour or so of faith sharing and planning. Be sure to invite each person face- to-face rather than via the phone or email. Your invitation might go something like this:

"Maria, I need your help with a very special project. I deeply appreciate all that you are doing for our ministry of (name of the ministry). I see in you a person of living faith, someone who makes sharing the Good News of Jesus a priority. You are just the right person to invite others into this ministry. Would you join me and a few others from the parish for shared food and conversation about this?"

If the volunteer asks for further clarification, be up front that you are asking him or her to be a Core Team member. If needed, clarify the commitment by saying that their obligation would be to come to the meeting, and, if they liked what they heard about the "mission," to invite two other people to become recruiters of other volunteers.

> **4 Steps of Recruiting**
> 1. **Select One Ministry for Recruitment**
> 2. **Parish Leaders Recruit the Core Team**
> 3. **Core Team Invites Recruiters**
> 4. **Recruiters Find Volunteers**

Open and close your meeting with prayer. During your meeting, share inspirational scripture passages about discipleship, and talk about what ignited your personal zeal for the Gospel. Ask your guests to talk about what has inspired their faith. Help them to see the power and joy that comes from living one's faith, and to connect that joy to the many works of discipleship performed in the parish. Don't rush over this step. Make sure that everyone is with you before you continue the process. Once you have established discipleship as a given, turn to the concrete task that you would like them to do. Invite them to be part of multiplying the ministry of the parish. Ask them to be your Core Team. Tell them that this phase of the process is simple, but not necessarily easy: you would like them to each find two people to recruit volunteers. Be clear that in addition to finding recruiters, you want your Core Team to provide encouragement and support to their recruiters.

To help them get a sense of the process, share a list of ideal qualities for a volunteer recruiter (SEE FIGURE 1, PAGE 19). Then lead a mini-brainstorming session of possible recruiters, using a master list of current or inactive volunteers. Who knows? You may surface enough names here to jump right into the work! Give them an outline of a process to use when enlisting recruiters. Finally, give them two dates: 1) a deadline, in one month's time, when they should turn in the names of their two recruits to you and 2) a check-in time, two weeks down the road, when they will report on their progress.

Conclude your meeting with an open invitation: are they are willing to take on this special assignment? If you sense hesitation in your group, tell them that you will call them the following day to discuss. Make sure that they take on this assignment willingly!

Step 3: Core Team Invites Recruiters

Goal: 8 to 10 Recruiters

In this phase, your Core Team gets to the work of finding recruiters. Keep the duration of the step to one month, so that it is intense and focused. For many the most productive time will be the first two weeks, when the team will approach the best candidates who spring to their minds.

The Core Team's Role in this Step

Core Team Members should keep their recruiting clear and simple:

1. Pray. Ask for the Spirit's inspiration in finding someone to do this ministry. Ask for what you need to invite people joyfully, from the heart.

2. Brainstorm. With a spouse or close friend from the parish, make a list of people who might be good recruiters. Do you know anyone who has shown an ability to reach out to others? This person need not be an extrovert; many strong

Introverts are comfortable relating one-to-one with people. There are a growing number of people who own their own home-based business. They are accustomed to inviting people to join them – this task could be a natural fit.

3. Verify. Pass your initial list by your parish leader. He or she can verify whether another member of the Core Team is recruiting people on your list already. Your leader might also be aware of why it would be particularly appropriate – or inappropriate – to issue the invitation now. It is a good idea to let the pastor/pastoral life director see the list as well, for the same reasons.

4. Invite. Set up a time to meet the potential recruiter. It would be best to make this invitation in person, say, after a Sunday Mass, but a phone call may be the only workable way to get through to them. Request some time to talk in person, either at one of your houses, at church, or even at a favorite coffee shop. if the potential volunteer presses you about why you want to meet in person rather than talk on the phone, tell the truth: you would like him or her to help you with an important church ministry, but would prefer to talk about it in person when you are both free of interruptions and distractions. If pressed further about the ministry, tell him or her that you think he or she is ideally suited to help grow the parish's ministry of (fill in the name) as a volunteer recruiter. However, do not let him or her give an immediate yes or no on the phone. Explain that you would like to explain the terms of the ministry fully in person.

5. Meet. Set up a private meeting with each of your potential recruiters. When you get together, start by sharing your own version of what sets your faith on fire, and why you think this parish ministry is important. Tell them why you agreed to be a member of the Core Team. Explain that just as your role is fixed for a set duration, you are inviting them to a role with a distinct beginning and end. You are asking them to be a recruiter of two parish volunteers.

To help them get a sense of the process, share the list of responsibilities of a volunteer recruiter and a list of ideal qualities for the volunteer ministries in question. Ask them if anyone comes to mind immediately as they look at these qualities. Then offer any other ideas that you have found helpful for recruiting. Finally, give them two dates: 1) a short Ministry Orientation session with the ministry leaders; and 2) a deadline when they should turn in names of people who have accepted their initial invitation to explore the ministry.

Conclude your meeting with the same open invitation that you received: are they are willing to take on this special assignment? If they need time to discern, set a time when you can call them to discuss it.

The Parish Leader's Role in This Step

As this level of recruiting you have several tasks to perform.

You will need to:

- Lead the screening of recruiters who have been generated by your Core Team.
- Serve as the parish representative to issue the direct invitation into the role of recruiting.
- Attend the Ministry Orientation meeting with Core Team Members and recruiters.
- Provide assistance for volunteer recruiters on the vision and the method of recruiting and monitor the progress of your Core Team and follow up with them after they are done this part of their work.

At the Ministry Orientation, provide a parish leader's perspective on the ministry, answer any follow up questions they might have, give them pointers on recruiting across the many levels of ministry, and, most important, drive home that central objective of instilling zeal for the mission.

Step 4: Recruiters Find Volunteers

Goal: 16 to 20 Volunteers

Take another look at that goal, and think about how a ministry will blossom with an infusion of up to 20 fresh volunteers. You can modify the goals as you see fit. However, if you plan to do this recruitment process every year, make sure that you limit it so that you actually have the resources to manage the people you get!

Ideal Qualities for a Volunteer Recruiter
Vibrant Faith
Enthusiasm for the Mission
Commitment to Service
Sense of Humor
Ability to talk with people

The Volunteer Recruiter's Role in this Step

Volunteer Recruiters should follow the same method that was worked for them:

1. Pray. Ask the Holy Spirit to inspire your work, and set you on fire with enthusiasm for the mission.

2. Learn. Take part in the Ministry Orientation. Learn all you can about various aspects of the ministry for which you are recruiting. Be sure to obtain a list of key volunteers whom you can call for further information or follow up.

3. Brainstorm. With a spouse or close friend from the parish, make a list of people who might be good volunteers in the ministry area. Think of people who might benefit from doing the ministry, as well as people who might have just the right skills or attitudes. Consider people who would benefit from the challenges or rewards of serving. Think outside of the box – who needs this gift of ministering to others right now?

4. Verify. Pass your initial list by your parish leader. He or She can verify whether another volunteer recruiter has already enlisted anyone on your list. Your leader should also pass the list by your pastor/pastoral life director, to ensure that it is appropriate to issue the invitation now.

5. Invite. Set up a time to meet the potential volunteer. Tell them up front that you think they will be uplifted by serving in the ministry of (insert the ministry name).

Request time to talk in person, either at one of your houses, at church, or even at a favorite coffee shop. Follow the same rules listed in other steps of this process: stress that you would like their undivided attention by meeting face-to-face.

6. Meet. Set up a private meeting with each of your potential volunteers. When you get together, start by sharing why the ministry for which you are recruiting is important to you. If you have served in the ministry, tell them what made it such a good experience. Tell them why you agreed to be a volunteer recruiter. Explain that just as your role is fixed for a set duration, you are inviting them to a role with a distinct beginning and end – a one year term.

Help them to get a sense of the process, and share the list of ministry levels and responsibilities. Then offer any other ideas that you have found helpful when you learned about the ministry.

7. Invite. Conclude your meeting with the same open invitation that you received: are they willing to consider this ministry for a year? Regardless of their answer, encourage them to attend the Ministry Orientation session. This is really important: Reassure them that while there are many different levels of commitment available for serving in the ministry, no one is going to pressure them into serving. If the individual states outright that they are not interested in volunteering, ask them if it would be okay touch base with them in another year. Use discretion and care here; do not badger them, as this is not a sales call.

8. Update. Provide your parish leader with a list of those who have accepted your invitation immediately, and those who are considering the invitation. Be sure to also convey the names of those who have declined your invitation, and your agreed upon timetable for follow up.

And What about the Rest of the parish?

How does this recruiting recruiters business activate the entire parish? The answer to the question lies in how often you use your Core Team and recruiters, and how you follow up with both groups.

Keep the working time of your Core Team and volunteer recruiters fixed and limited. Once they are done with their task after a month or so, cut them free for the year. Better yet, cut them free entirely, as you allow them to only work as recruiters once. Getting a fresh batch of Core Team members and volunteer recruiters each year will quickly disperse the recruiting spirit into your parish community. It is tempting to keep people on board who know how the process works, particularly if they are eager and open to repeating their job the next year. But the more new people you surface and personally call forward, the greater the benefit.

Letting these volunteers serve only once doesn't mean that you will lose them. If they are zealous about the mission, they will do other things. They will also have a "recruiting eye." After each group of recruiter has completed its assignments, bring them together for a follow up gathering. Ask them for insights, for people and ideas that caught their attention throughout the recruiting experience. Thank them for helping you with this year's recruitment, and ask them to continue to have eyes/ears for people who would be wonderful ministers throughout the many levels of your program. Keep an email list of all "alums" in this group, and periodically send them electronic feelers for fresh faces and new names. You will eventually have friends from throughout the parish sending you the name of this or that parishioner as a potential match for ministry. This is the long-term method for multiplying ministry.

Chris' Soapbox #897: The True Meaning of Delegation

Many years ago, I knew a catechetical leader who had a reputation as a master delegator. Her peers were amazed at how she was able to get volunteers to serve as lead catechists, coordinators of various components, and even administrators of entire program nights. We were astonished at how well she was making the delegator's slogan "Work yourself out of a job!" a reality. However, we discovered another reality soon after she retired. The leader who took the helm after her found the parish programs in a shambles. There was chaos, disorder and confusion, and the quality of the program had sunk so low that he had to step in and take the helm at every level. To all of us who were peers in ministry, it seemed that the lofty goal of "working ourselves out of a job" had been pitched off a cliff.

The moral of this story is a warning for all of us in ministry. Being a parish leader is not about "working yourself out of a job." Yes, delegation of tasks is a way of empowering your volunteers, and spreading the work around. Yes, it is also a way to draw more people into ministry. However, effective delegation ends when the leader loses sight of the vision, commitment, and skill sets of the volunteers. A number of us who witnessed the implosion of our colleague's program observed that, in many places, key volunteers had been given roles for which they were not adequately trained or oriented to the mission. The roles that counted here were leadership roles – ones that the catechetical leader should have surrendered only after much more deliberation and training.

There is no shortcut in this process, and it is often frustrating. You may get a volunteer fully oriented to take over a certain aspect of ministry, just as he announces he is moving to another state. You may spend countless hours grooming another who has the ideal skill set for leadership, only to find that she isn't interested in ministry anymore. These are times when you can either 1) pull out your hair and rend your garments or 2) say a prayer to the Holy Spirit, trust that the Spirit knows what the Spirit is doing, and begin anew.

Don't even think about working yourself out of a job when you delegate. On the contrary, you must remain active and attentive throughout the entire process. If you are afraid of taking on more work, you had better flee from the ministry! Keep this in mind as we move through the recruitment process and on to discernment and training.

Person-to-Person Recruiting = Jesus-Style Recruiting

A leader calls together a small band of Core Team members, and prepares them to in turn invite others to join the cause of spreading the Good News. Does it not have a nice Gospel ring to it? The more you make recruiting about face-to-face encounter, and passing on the joy and light of the message to the next person, the more you recruit as Jesus did.

The Recruiting Structure

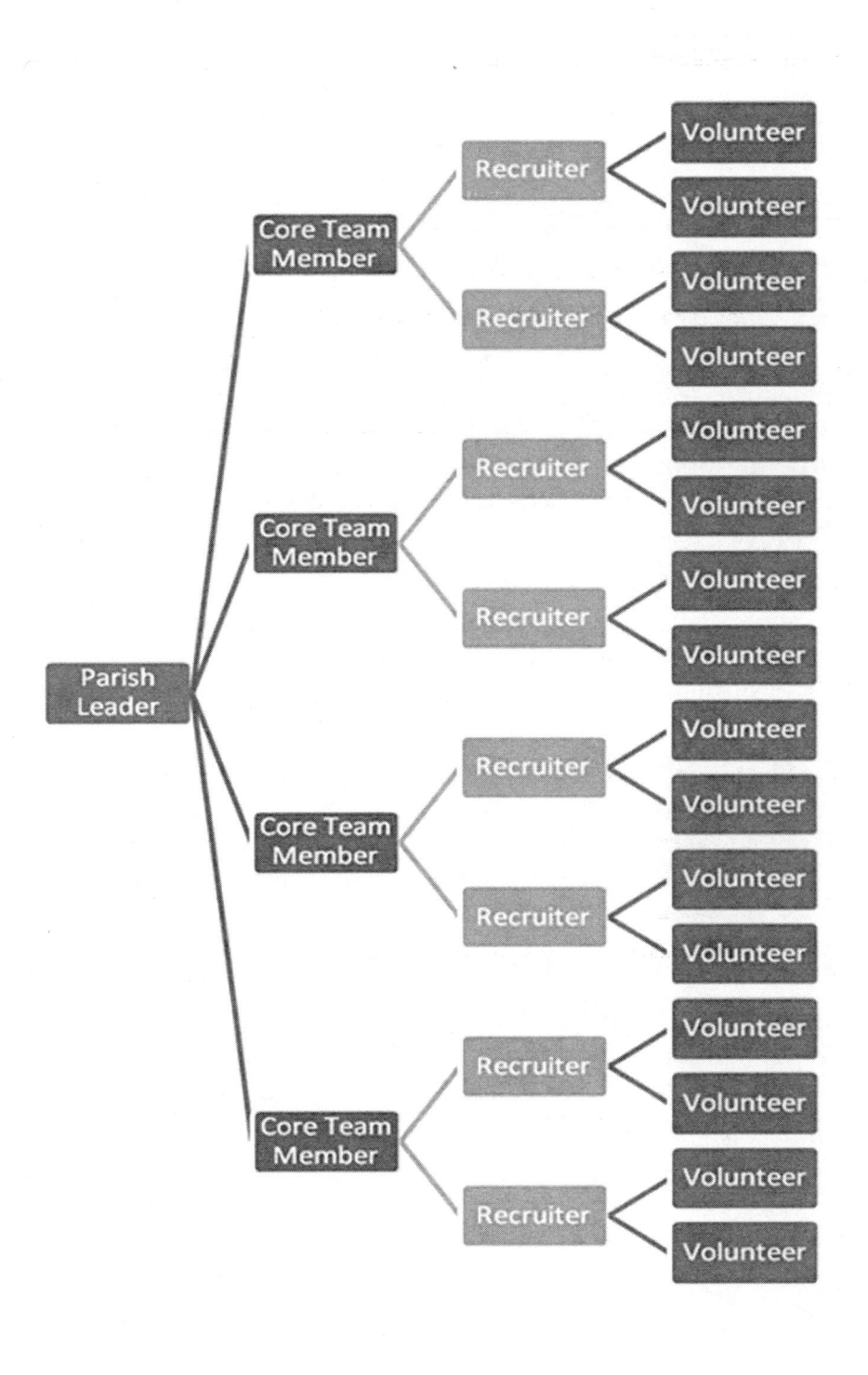

```
Parish Leader
├── Core Team Member
│   ├── Recruiter
│   │   ├── Volunteer
│   │   └── Volunteer
│   └── Recruiter
│       ├── Volunteer
│       └── Volunteer
├── Core Team Member
│   ├── Recruiter
│   │   ├── Volunteer
│   │   └── Volunteer
│   └── Recruiter
│       ├── Volunteer
│       └── Volunteer
├── Core Team Member
│   ├── Recruiter
│   │   ├── Volunteer
│   │   └── Volunteer
│   └── Recruiter
│       ├── Volunteer
│       └── Volunteer
└── Core Team Member
    ├── Recruiter
    │   ├── Volunteer
    │   └── Volunteer
    └── Recruiter
        ├── Volunteer
        └── Volunteer
```

Chapter 4

Go Face-to-Face

An in-person invitation is not just the best strategy for recruitment; it is Gospel Evangelization at work. Here's why we need to meet people face-to-face, and some dos and don'ts for these face-to-face encounters.

In my view, we started to lose it with instant-on television. You remember instant-on television, don't you? If you are a Baby-Boomer or older, you can go even farther than that; you remember a time before instant-on television. For those of you born in the 70's and later, here's what I mean.

I grew up in the 60's, when television was just coming into its own. Back in those days (What a hoot it is to say that!), TVs were not really black-and-white; it is more accurate to say that they were black-and-green. It was kind of a drab, grayish-green at that. The other interesting feature about early televisions is that they took forever to warm up. After you turned them on, the screen lit up from the middle and the glow spread to the outer edges. If you had any signal to speak of, the screen gradually coalesced so that you could see the action, but you always heard the audio first. After the amazing breakthrough of true black-and-white screens, the next innovation I remember was the instant-on television. As long as it had electricity, the machine could give you both audio and video the moment you turned it on. Instant-on came of age, and the world of electronics would never be the same.

> **Jesus-Style Recruitment Tip #4:**
> **Look them in the eye.**
>
> Jesus, looking at him, loved him and said, 'You lack one thing; go, sell what you own, and give the money to the poor, and you will have treasure in heaven; then come, follow me. - Mark 10:21

Today everything is instant-on, or better said, always on. Electronic communication is instantaneous. With mobile technology, we also take everything with us. We are a hair's breadth away from an age where anyone can get hold of anyone, anywhere, at anytime…instantly. Without waiting we can jot off a quick email or text message. We can talk to our cousin Reilly while he is hiking in Oregon, or immediately inform "friends" on any number of social networking sites that we are buying liverwurst at a particularly good deli. Very soon we will have difficulty remembering what it was like to call someone without live video.

While these astonishing advancements in communication bring numerous blessings and conveniences, they have also brought us closer and closer to losing something precious. Following right behind the lost art of writing letters, I am afraid that we are rapidly losing the art of face-to-face communication. There is no adequate substitute for live and in person conversation. For the purposes of this book, this is not just a matter of best practices in recruitment; face-to-face and in person communication is about ministry.

Yes, we are talking about a METHOD

Try this exercise when you are sitting down for a cup of coffee or tea with a friend:

Without explaining why, set a timer for two minutes. Ask the friend for those two minutes to converse without looking at you, perhaps even with the two of you back-to-back. After two minutes, reset the timer and have resume talking. After the timer has gone off the second time, ask your friend what he or she noticed over the past four minutes. If you can get past the strangeness of turning around and timing the conversation, I am sure you will note the obvious difference in quality between the two segments.

What do you get with in-person communication? Notice all of the facial cues, the body language, and the gestures. In conversation we engage with our eyes, our mouths, pats on the hand or whacking objects for emphasis. A conversation is like a symphony; the voice carries the melody and non-verbal cues strike up the harmony, chorus and counter-melodies. Sometimes the most amazing and moving parts of a conversation involve no spoken words at all.

Is it any wonder that the business world places such high value on "face time" with clients? Face-to-face conversation is the best medium for building a relationship with someone, and building relationships is how you ultimately build your business. Take away all of the in-person elements except for the voice (as in a phone conversation) and the symphony plays like a lone melody; it is nowhere near as rich and meaningful. Take it another step. Remove the spoken voice, and what remains? A written "chat," text, or email. While the written word is very useful for many types of communication, it is the least effective way to build a relationship with someone. It is not only missing all of the symphonic elements that so effectively convey thoughts, emotions and shared experiences; it also involves a time lag that bogs down the process.

Some might argue that video calling is pretty close to in-person conversation. It is, after all, face-to-face! While this medium adds warmth and dimension to a conversation, it just isn't the same as "being there." There are still miles and miles between you and the other person, both physically and figuratively. I use video calling at home with many members of my family. While we all enjoy the conversations much more than audio-only calls, that small screen and camera can't come close to replacing the magic that happens when my family members stand in a room together, share memories or a great story, laugh together, cry together, all at once, pray in silence, and, of course, share a touch, a punch on the arm, a hug.

Am I implying that in order to recruit volunteers for ministry we must only meet with them in-person, and never use the phone or other electronic means to share the Good News with them? Certainly not! However, I believe that just as the Church's social teaching includes a "preferential option for the poor," we must exercise a similar "preferential option" for face-to-face and in-person communication with those to whom we minister.

...but we must make it a MINDSET...

When considering options for communicating with others, get into the habit of choosing the most personal mode first. This would be a great Lenten or New Year's resolution. Use in-person contact instead of email to meet people on their turf and enter into their world. Make sure you look them in the eye! Make it a habit and work your way out of the so-called "convenient" modes of communication, one email and phone call at a time.

> **While I have regretted any number of emails that I have sent over the years, I have regretted very few face-to-face conversations.**

Start with this new mindset in your everyday life. Begin each day by resolving that you will respond to two emails or phone messages directly in person. Then look for ways to get those two encounters in. I have found this very rewarding. While I have regretted any number of emails that I have sent over the years, I have regretted very few face-to-face conversations. As much as I use email every day, I find it notoriously prone to misunderstanding. So many times others read a "tone" into my emails that I neither feel nor intend to convey. Often I have begun to reply to an inquiry by email, only to realize that my written response was so complicated that the recipient would never understand what I was trying to say. Solution #1? A phone call. An even better solution? An in-person conversation.

Carry this mindset into your parish's recruiting efforts as well. Where possible, use phone calls to set up face-to-face encounters. Use the "face time" to convey your love and enthusiasm for the ministry, and to discern your recruit's reaction to the call. Here's where paying attention to facial cues and body language come in! Make their time worthwhile by being prepared and organized. Show that you value the individuals with whom you meet by actively listening to them and being open to what you have to learn from them.

...and a MINISTRY

In-person communication is not just a great business method, or a helpful mindset. It is a ministry. It is not just ministry, but it is ministry the way Jesus did ministry. Is there any question that face-to-face was the way Jesus recruited disciples? We know he didn't have email and a cell phone. Many different scriptural accounts describe Jesus walking up to a would-be follower and saying, "Come!" He didn't sit around waiting for people to come to him. He preached in synagogues, in the Temple, and on hillsides. He went out to where the ordinary people lived, and walked among them. He met them where they were, and called them deeper...often one-by-one. He asked his disciples to do the same.

Some Implications of This Method for Our Recruiting Ministry

1. It must be *personal*. Despite the throngs that often followed Jesus, he always made time for individuals, whether it was the blind man Bartimaeus (Mark 10:46-52), children (Matthew 19:13-15), the woman caught in the act of adultery (John 8:1-11), or even a Roman soldier (Matthew 8:5-13). We must think about this process as a privileged opportunity to open the window of faith in our lives and the lives of those whom we recruit. We must try to make one-on-one meetings a higher priority than group meetings. We must surrender convenience for relationship-building.

2. Our recruiting must also *evangelize*. When we recruit as Jesus did we accept them right where they are, and we share our personal story of faith. We inspire others to volunteer not with a sense of guilt or obligation, but with an eager anticipation to experience what we have experienced through the gift of service.

3. Our recruiting must *challenge* . Jesus never kept the status quo. He goaded the keepers of the Law to a deeper, more spiritual sense of the Law. He exhorted sinners to leave their way of sin and walk the path of righteousness. He shook up the complacent to rethink their strategy of seeking the easy way. If we follow Jesus' example, we will invite potential recruits into a daring and bold adventure, which will stretch them and transform them.

4. Finally, our recruiting must be *authentic*. Jesus knew who he was and what he wanted. He knew how to talk about the Kingdom in everyday language that his listeners would understand. We must invite others to a faith we practice and a ministry we believe in. We must show how to serve by our authentic service. We must show them the benefits of volunteering by witnessing to the benefits we have reaped from ministering.

Some Face-to-Face Dos and Don'ts

Setting the life's work of Jesus as our model for volunteer recruitment can lead to setting some very lofty goals. This is fine, as long as we remember that Jesus is not only fully divine, but fully human! He worked within the limits of the world around him. He also recognized the fears and foibles of the motley band of followers who would later lead the early Church. With this in mind here are some practical do's and don'ts for in-person recruiting.

DON'T force the face-to-face encounter. As important as in-person contact is, there will be times when it simply won't be feasible. Some volunteers may be uncertain about meeting. Be willing to have a phone conversation instead. However, make an appointment for the call, so that the recruit will be able to free himself or herself from potential distractions.

DON'T keep the meeting agenda a secret. When I am approached by someone who wants to meet with me but won't tell me what the agenda is, I get very uneasy. If your recruit wants to know what the meeting topic is, tell him or her that his or her name has surfaced as a person who would be very well suited to (name the ministry), and that you would like to discuss this further. If the volunteer asks why you can't discuss it on the phone, simply suggest that this is an invitation you really want to give face-to-face, and you would like some time to discern this topic with him or her.

DON'T promise too much too soon. Let's say that you call a woman in your parish to set up a meeting about being a volunteer, and she says immediately, "Say no more! I'd love to! When do we start?" You will likely feel the urge to say, "Okay, let's go!" to her. Resist it! Set up the time to meet and talk. Together sift through details, pray, and discern. With all cases, allow time for the Holy Spirit to help you and the recruits match up their gifts with the right parish ministry.

DON'T grill the recruits. Hopefully your face-to-face meeting will be the first of several. You don't need to cover soup-to-nuts. Think of your meeting as a kitchen-table-cup-of-coffee meeting, a relaxing conversation. Take time to enjoy it, and get to know the potential volunteer.

DON'T kill too many trees, but *DO prepare handouts.* Compile a "job description" for key volunteer positions, develop notes about how your program works, and provide a summary of what the volunteer should do next after the meeting. It might also be nice to have your parish mission statement, or another type of vision statement handy. Keep the number of pages low, but have key elements on the handouts so that you don't have to say everything at the first meeting.

DO pray together. A short opening prayer, as simple as "Come, Holy Spirit – inspire our time together!" may do just fine if you are meeting at the local coffee shop or another public place. Be sure to take a few more moments at the end to offer a prayer of gratitude. I have often found this to be the most amazing part of the meeting. Lead the prayer, but allow a moment for your recruit to pray, too. If he or she doesn't wish to pray, you will have a nice moment of silence, which speaks fine for itself.

DO allow your faith to come through. Share elements of your personal story of faith, without being maudlin or monopolizing the conversation. When you share your convictions, look the other person earnestly in the eye. Ask the Holy Spirit to let your joy and love be evident in what you say.

DO take time to listen. Be sure to take as much time to listen as to talk. Take active interest in what your recruit is saying.

DO take notes. It is fine to bring a pad of paper to jot down notes about your conversation. I know that I am lost without them later! Write simple phrases to jog your memory later, like "enjoys reading," "likes Fr. K's homilies," "Chemistry degree," etc.

DO write a summary of the meeting afterwards. After your recruit leaves, write down your impressions of the visit, and what struck you the most. This will be useful for your later discernment and follow up.

I suppose I do not have to add this, but I will. Take care to keep your notes or anything you have written about this interview private and confidential. Just because the notes are on your desk does not always mean they are not viewed by others.

Chapter 5
Truth That Sells

Don't just tell the whole truth about the commitment involved; Sell the whole truth. Here's how to capture the imagination of volunteer catechists through your love for ministry.

The television ad goes something like this:

A middle-aged woman looks very pensive as she lies in bed at the end of the day. She says to her husband, "He wants to join the Army." The husband replies, "He wants to make a difference." "Are you okay with it?" she says. He replies, "Do we have a choice?"

There is a long pause, and then the husband says, "We'll discuss it more in the morning."

The camera zooms out, and as the image fades a caption says, "It is a difficult decision. Discuss it."

I saw this remarkable commercial last night, and marveled at how well it fit into the process of volunteer recruitment. It "works" on so many different levels:

> **Jesus-Style Recruitment Tip #5:Inspire them with the Truth.**
>
> "If you continue in my word, you are truly my disciples; and you will know the truth, and the truth will make you free." - John 8:31-32

1. It is honest and straightforward. It brings one of the key issues with military service front and center, namely, parental concern for the safety of their children.

2. It doesn't minimize the commitment or cost. It acknowledges up front that this is not an easy undertaking.

3. It invites discernment. Rather than following a typical Madison Avenue rush to the quick sell, it encourages potential recruits to seriously consider whether the task is right for them.

4. It issues a challenge. The commercial turns the greatest roadblock from a liability into an asset. The hard work and risk of military service is touted as the very reason why people should volunteer!

This is not just a clever advertising ploy. This commercial contains many of the elements that we should use when we take Jesus-Style Recruiting seriously. It very poignantly uses the truth to sell the message. We can do this, too. You don't have to trick your volunteers into ministry. Let's apply the attributes of this ad to our recruiting efforts, and then consider one overarching method for "selling" your volunteer ministry.

Be Honest and Straightforward about the Cost

Jesus was specific to his followers about the cost of ministry: "They will hand you over to councils and flog you in their synagogues; and you will be dragged before governors and kings because of me, as a testimony to them and the Gentiles... Brother will betray brother to death, and a father his child, and children will rise against parents and have them put to death; and you will be hated by all because of my name. But the one who endures to the end will be saved. " (Matthew 10:17-18,21-22)

> **Honesty up front is both truer to the Gospel message and of greater benefit to building the ministry.**

Jesus did not just invite his followers to die to self. Despite his clear warnings that discipleship could mean persecution or death, they still came!

Following this precedent our task looks relatively simple. After all, we don't have to add "willingness to die" onto the volunteer's job description! If we have truly "leveled" our program as described earlier in this book, potential volunteers can weigh multiple levels of commitment. Just the same, I am sure many of you reading this book worry that being honest about the commitment will lead to dozens of volunteers at the lower levels, and just a handful at the more demanding levels. I have good news: if this happens to you, you will find yourself in the glad company of Jesus and his disciples. There will always be less people working at the deepest levels of your mission. The trick is to recruit those people in such a way that they stay with it as long as possible.

Spell out the expectations for all of your ministries clearly. Write out job descriptions that include the time commitment, responsibilities, and training needed. If those requirements keep too many people away, find creative ways to break them down into simpler or less burdensome parts.

Many of us who have served in church ministry share the common stories of being "tricked" into ministry. We were told "it won't take too long," or "all the work is done for you in the book," or "we just need someone to turn on the lights and get everyone going each week," or any number of half-truths to get us in the door. The fact that you are reading this chapter suggests that this recruiting ploy worked on you. Your recruiter may well have seen a "spark of the Spirit" in you that inspired him or her to call you to ministry. However, I believe that honesty up front is both truer to the Gospel message and of greater benefit to building the ministry.

Invite Discernment

Notice the numerous references in the Gospels about Jesus retreating to pray. Throughout his ministry he stops to pray, reflect, and surrender his life to God's will. This could be no clearer the night before his death, when he prays outside the city: "He came out and went, as was his custom, to the Mount of Olives; and the disciples followed him. When he reached the place, he said to them, 'Pray that you may not come into the time of trial.' Then he withdrew from them about a stone's throw, knelt down, and prayed, 'Father, if you are willing, remove this cup from me; yet, not my will but yours be done.' Then an angel from heaven appeared to him and gave him strength. In his anguish he prayed more earnestly, and his sweat became like great drops of blood falling down on the ground." – Luke 22:39-44

After this he sets out on his journey to the Cross with calm resolution, knowing that this is the right thing to do. Luke notes in the first verse that is was Jesus' "custom" to go out to the Mount of Olives to pray. His whole life and ministry is framed by taking regular time apart to prayerfully hand his life over to the will of his Father.

We should not overlook the fact that he takes forty days to pray and fast before beginning his ministry (See the accounts in Luke 4, Matthew 4, and Mark 1). If we believe that volunteer ministries are of vital importance to the life of the Church, and if we believe that God calls us to this work, then we must allow time for potential volunteers, especially those we are inviting into the more involved ministries, to pray and listen for that call. When we ask them to stop, pray, and reflect before responding to our invitation, we signal our profound respect for both the potential minister and the ministry.

Don't snatch up volunteers before they can change their minds. Set a policy, and make a list of key ministries into which you will never accept people after the very first visit. Give them time, or better, make them take time, to pray and think it over. Set a follow up visit for a week later. Give them materials to guide their prayer and reflection. Don't be afraid to invite discernment.

Issue a Challenge

The cost of ministry is closely related to the challenge of ministry. However, the two are not the same. The cost, or price you have to pay, is almost always perceived as something negative. This is not so with the challenge. How many times have you heard someone say they are doing something, whether it is taking on the New York Times Crossword Puzzle, hiking that tall mountain, reading a difficult book, starting an intricate hobby, or taking on a new job, "for the challenge" of it? Challenges inspire us. We shake our heads in amazement at people around us who grab the bull by the horns and try something difficult. Don't be afraid to advertise these ministries as challenging. However, make sure that you do so in a way that not only keeps the challenge *distinct* from the cost, but also helps the recruit see that the challenge *outweighs* the cost. It will be simplest to illustrate this with a fictional example.

Sam is trying to recruit a catechist to teach various doctrinal sessions for the catechumenate. From an initial contact on the phone he gets a sense that Carmella might be a good match for the ministry. When they meet to discuss the ministry further, Sam describes it this way:

Sam and Carmella, Take 1

"Carmella, let me start by giving you more details about the position. As an RCIA catechist, you would be responsible for teaching a one hour session about once a month, perhaps more if we don't get enough catechists. Many catechists have said that it usually takes them at least two hours to prepare a one hour session. Since we are asking you to teach doctrine to adults, your preparation time could very well be longer. The facilitator of the group will lead a lectionary-based prayer and reflection for about 20 minutes at the beginning, but the rest of the time is yours.

We would like you to incorporate at least 30-40 minutes of input for that session, plus moments for large and small group faith-sharing, reflection and guided discussion of the readings for each meeting. You can do other types of activities and use media if you wish. You will be using the text and corresponding elements in the *Catechism of the Catholic Church* and the Bible. This is a lot of work, but other catechists would be here to help you, as am I. I invite you to speak to the catechists who are already involved. They find it very rewarding."

While Sam can be lauded for following the spirit of truth-in-advertising, I don't think his pitch is going to be too successful. What he is doing wrong here is leading with the cost. In the world of sales, this would be a huge no-no. Unless you are sure that the cost you are advertising is so good that it is of clear benefit to the consumer, do not mention the price first. What you should mention first is all of the reasons why the consumer would want to buy the product. This is where the challenge comes in. See what you think of Sam's approach in this example.

Sam and Carmella, Take 2

"Carmella, thanks so much for agreeing to meet with me again. Allow me to introduce Janice. As I mentioned on the phone, I asked her to join us today so you could hear more about the catechist position from someone who is already doing it. I have asked her to talk about how she has been personally challenged and inspired by the work. She can also give you real pointers about what is involved with preparing each session."

"Hi, Carmella, nice to meet you. I was excited to hear that someone else might be joining us as a catechist for the catechumenate. I know that if God calls you to this ministry, you will find it as rewarding as I have. Sam isn't kidding about the challenge. I was very daunted when I first thought about leading sessions with other adults. But I have been amazed at this experience. When I prepare for a session, I read through the material, and I look at the corresponding sections of the *Catechism of the Catholic Church*. Often I am startled by things that I didn't know before. Many of us catechists say that we learn twice as much as we teach! Our faith is so rich and so deep. Our catechumens and their godparents come with a lot of great questions, and there are times where I have to tell them that I don't know the answer. That's when I come to Sam, or go back to the material. And I always bring back the answer. This experience stretches me, and teaches me so much about my faith. I have learned that being a catechist is not so about being willing to teach, but being willing to learn. That is both humbling...and uplifting!"

Yes, I cheated in the second scenario by allowing Sam to bring in a testimonial. Inviting someone to tell their story in the first person is powerful. Besides that change, did you notice the shift in emphasis? Janice does not minimize the hard work involved with being a catechist. However, she does not lead with it. As a matter of fact, most of the cost-related details are not in the monologue at all, but are presumably saved for the "Q & A" later in the conversation.

Janice opened with the challenge. She demonstrated how the "daunting" work led her to satisfying insights about her faith, and enjoyable interaction with other adults even when their questions were beyond her.

Before you begin to "sell" any ministry in your parish, clarify the challenge it offers. What benefits might the volunteer gain by doing it? How might it help the volunteer to grow personally, spiritually, physically, mentally? What skill will it lead the volunteer to perfect? What personal accomplishment might the volunteer achieve, or what height might he or she reach by doing this?

Promoting your most difficult ministries through their challenges will lead to great things. By contrast, promoting these same ministries with an "anyone can do it" strategy will lead to shoddy ministry and dissatisfied ministers.

It Is All about the Benefits

Telling the truth about ministry is not the only component we need to be effective recruiters. Jesus never lied, but he used much more than the cold bare facts to inspire disciples to ministry. As Number One Salesman for the Reign of God, he sold the people on the *benefits* of living the Good News. He promised them eternal life (John 3:15-16)]. He told them they would be blessed and happy (Luke 6:19-27). He reassured them of the guidance and strength of the Spirit (John 16:1-15). Jesus promised his followers a permanent home with the Father (John 14:2). They would experience the gifts of his light and peace (Luke 1:78-79), and, despite the hardships of Gospel living, his followers would ultimately find his yoke easy, and his burden light (Matthew 11:29-30)]. We will fall short of the Master's call if we offer anything less to our volunteers.

In Church circles, we rarely promote the benefits of our programs. We usually just describe them, or list their features. Let's close out this chapter with a couple more takes. Fr. Bob has stood up at the end of mass for announcements. Like Sam, he too is making a quick pitch for new catechists:

Fr. Bob, Take 1

Fr. Bob: I would like to issue a special plea for help with our catechetical program. This is a very important ministry in our parish. Catechists are needed for grades 4, 5, and 6. If we can't find catechists for these grades we not be able to run them. I myself plan to teach once a month. Won't you join me in this ministry, please? The classes that are available run for one hour three times a month. See me or Mrs. Ketcham after mass if you are interested. Please help our children!

Fr. Bob, Take 2

Fr. Bob: Are you looking for a fresh and inspiring way to grow in your faith? Are you looking for a meaningful and enjoyable way to help others? Ask Joe and Cindy Munion about what they are doing to "jump start" their faith. They are catechists! When I asked them what brings them back year after year to serving as 6th grade catechists, they said it was "because we learn so much more than we teach." And they are teaching 6th grade! Consider joining them and many others in this challenging but deeply rewarding ministry. We need you – we need catechists for at least three grades. See me or Mrs. Ketcham after mass if you would like to help with this ministry.

Take 1 is what we encounter most in our parishes. We simply describe, announce, and then throw in a bit of Catholic guilt on the end! I hope that you notice the difference in Take 2. Fr. Bob is not just stating the need and describing the features and cost; he is clearly describing the benefits for the volunteer. Notice the shift from doing it "for the children" in Take 1 to doing it for their own benefit in Take 2. He emphasis is not "This is what you *must* do for this ministry" (the cost), rather "This is what you will *get* from doing this ministry" (the benefits). This is a shift in emphasis, not truth. By all means, be truthful as you are "selling" your programs. However, you must at the same time frame every pitch that you make using the following self-assessment: What would convince *me* to do this ministry? How is this benefiting not just the recipients, but the volunteers themselves? Think benefits, not features; think inspirational challenges, not daunting costs. Above all, think of calling people to authentic discipleship through ministry. Don't be afraid to tell the truth, but yes, heed the advice to Jesus to be "wise as serpents and innocent as doves." (Matthew 10:16)

Chapter 6

Discern the Gifts

It is time to dig into the work of formation. Ask the Holy Spirit to guide your discernment when you meet potential volunteers. Use Interviews to determine their entry level job, and the training they need to do it. Then draw them deeper.

Conventional wisdom suggests that we recruit volunteers, place them in ministries, and then form them. Jesus-Style Recruiting should make it clear that the entire process is formation, from steps 1 to 100. From the moment Jesus first met potential disciples, whether he was teaching by the seashore, walking through the crowds, or calling them by name, he began forming them to become bearers of the Good News. Be sure to frame your ministry that way as well.

Volunteer recruitment seems to have gotten more and more difficult over the years. The pool of potential volunteers appears to be shrinking...and those who do volunteer are busier and busier. How do we engage them, and keep them engaged?

> **Jesus-Style Recruitment Tip #6: Help them follow their joy.**
> "Ask and you will receive, so that your joy may be complete."
> - John 16.24

After twenty years in the field, I am happy to announce that I have found the secret. (It has actually been woven throughout preceding chapters, so you shouldn't be surprised as I spell it out here.)

When I was in my 20's, I met regularly with a priest who served as my spiritual director. On one occasion I asked him if he had any suggestions for how I should discern my vocation. He amazed me with his instant response. He said, "Yes, I do, Christ." (He was French Canadian, and he never quite figured out the shortening of Christopher to Chris.) "It is simple. Just follow your joy."

Follow Your Joy

I have repeated this mantra for years. I have applied it to myriads of situations. It is most appropriate when applied to ministry. This is the key to enlivening your volunteers: match them with ministries that give them a deep sense of satisfaction, and guide them into a God-connection that gives them joy. This is the heart of discernment.

Discernment When You Meet Someone for the First Time

Jesus was a master at reading people. He sized up people in the first few moments after meeting them. He recognized Philip as a true Israelite (John 1:47-50);

he knew the judgmental thoughts of the scribes when he forgave the paralyzed man (Matthew 9:4); he sensed the deep faith of the Canaanite woman (Matthew 15:28), the Centurion (Matthew 8:10) and Zacchaeus the tax collector (Luke 19:5). Jesus had a knack for calling people to whatever action was appropriate for their level of faith. Most of the time, he simply called them to love more, and live righteously, within their current station of life. He called just a select few to full-time active ministry.

In the same manner, you can size people up when you meet them. Some might argue that you lack Jesus' gift of discernment because you are not divine. However, you have the gift of the Holy Spirit, poured out in your heart, to lead you. In his list of spiritual gifts, St. Paul includes the "discernment of spirits" (I Corinthians 12: 10). St. Paul may have had another definition in mind, but I don't think it would be stretching too far to think of this gift as discerning how the Holy Spirit is working in someone's life. Ask the Holy Spirit for the gift of discernment of spirits as you recruit volunteers. Presume in faith that you will receive this gift. However, remember that none of the Spirit's gifts reside in just one or two individuals. To keep a balanced perspective, make sure that there are others charged with this task of discernment as well. This could include members of your staff, an advisory board, or seasoned volunteers. I will offer some suggestions how to disperse this responsibility below.

Ask the Spirit to guide you when you first meet someone. Encourage all of your volunteers to do this as well. Get into the practice of silently praying, "Holy Spirit, how are you calling this person to serve you?" Start with the presumption that the Holy Spirit is calling them right where they are, to bring the Good News into their current workplace, household, or school. Accept this as their primary, and most important calling. Then, ask the Spirit if there might be some additional role for this person in the formal work of the Church.

In many cases, you will know from your first meeting that a prospective volunteer should start as a Level One Provider or as a Level Two Helper, giving discrete moments of service to the Church. These people might be aloof, looking simply to be served rather than to serve. Your immediate challenge will be to consider whether they are aloof because they are not interested in getting involved, or because they are quiet and reserved. It is hazardous to presume too much too soon! When in doubt, it is best not to demand too much. You need not discern any further with them, at least not immediately. Give them a chance to get the lay of the land, with a minimum degree of commitment.

In a similar manner, placing a Professional Career Volunteer may require nothing more than your initial meeting. Often professionals will volunteer their services right at the start. If you can find a meaningful way to use their skills, do so right away, particularly if they demonstrate their effectiveness by example or by showing products they have made. At the same time, take note of any skills that they exercise in their professional careers which apply directly to the parish's higher levels of ministry.

When you meet people whom you consider for Level 4 Semi-skilled and Level 5 Skilled volunteers, move with caution. Not everyone who says they would like to be a skilled volunteer will be qualified for it. At the same time, others whom you tap for skilled ministry will have no clue what you see in them. These two levels of recruitment require additional discernment.

Start with the Ministry Orientation meeting that we discussed earlier. In addition to a broad overview of the many levels of ministry, offer time to break out into smaller sections for specifics about the skilled and semi-skilled ministries. You might even want to make it possible for a potential volunteer to attend information sessions about more than one ministry.

> **This meeting is as much about inspiration as it is about information.**

This meeting is as much about inspiration as it is about information. Invite one or two of your volunteers to share their personal experience of the ministry, with emphasis on the reward of volunteering. Invite participants to reflect upon what gives them a sense of satisfaction and joy. As you then share the roles and tasks associated with the ministry, encourage them to think about the personal benefit they would get from volunteering. Jump start their discernment by inviting them to reflect on whether they can see themselves doing the ministry. During the meeting, pay attention to participants' reactions. Do they "get" the vision behind the ministry? Are they keenly interested? You should be able to discern some of this from both their spoken words and their body language. Are they leaning into the conversation, or sitting back with their arms crossed? Are they asking questions? If the Ministry Orientation stirs someone to volunteer, invite him or her to meet with you privately for an interview. Leaders working with just a few volunteers at a time might combine the Orientation with the interview. If you do this, be sure to leave yourself plenty of extra time!

The Interview: A Faith Conversation

While the term "interview" is apt for this type one-on-one meeting, a parish volunteer interview differs greatly from a conventional job interview. Unlike the job interview, this is not simply a matter of someone applying for one position. As the interviewer, your job is not just to give thumbs-up or thumbs-down to one position, but to match the candidate's gifts, skills and desires with a ministry or ministries. You are both job coach and hiring agent! Another way in which a volunteer ministry interview differs from a job interview is the content. Your interview should follow the format of a faith conversation. Both words – "faith" and "conversation" – are important.

Your interview is about faith. It is about how God is already at work in the potential volunteer's life; it is about where God is calling him or her now. Presume that faith has brought the volunteer to this moment, and that God's grace has already done amazing things in his or her life. One way to start might be to ask, "What brought you here today? Beyond the direct invitation from a friend or member of the church (or me!), what prompted you to consider volunteering in church ministry?" You could also start with, "Tell me a bit about your faith journey. What have been some of the blessings along the way? What have been some of the challenges to your faith?" With little prompting, some people will easily launch into their faith story after this. However, others may need more encouragement to share. Often volunteers come forward because of their children, or another family member who has had a significant faith experience. Questions about family life are great fodder for conversation.

This leads us to the second word: "conversation." Your interview should be a two-way exchange, and you should actively participate in it. This means that it is appropriate for you to share elements of your personal faith journey with the potential volunteer. However, don't forget that this interview isn't about you! Limit your participation to around twenty-five percent of the talking and seventy-five percent of the active listening. There are numerous techniques attached to the concept of active listening, but the main idea is taking personal interest in what the interviewee is saying, and making this clear to him or her by the way that you respond. After you have invited your interviewee to share a little about his or her faith journey, describe a part of your own story that is similar. However, these are busy people and you do not need to go on and on about yourself.

"I know what you mean. I felt liberated when I went to college and could decide on my own whether to go to church. As I look back on it today, I think that I kept it up even when I didn't feel like going, because my parents had helped me to learn that it was an important part of my life."

Ask clarifying questions, or simply invite the interviewee to tell you more:
"I am puzzled by that statement. What makes you say that your wife has more faith than you do?"

Summarize what they have shared with you in your own words:

"Though you wonder what the future will bring, you have clearly seen God working in your past, even amidst some difficult trials. Do I have that right?"

This is a conversation with a purpose, so you must also actively listen for signs of ministry. As you listen, prayerfully ask yourself where God is working, and even speaking in the interviewee's life. Enjoy this opportunity to get to know someone a little bit better, and give thanks for the privilege of meeting them at this point along the faith journey.

The Interview as Spiritual Direction?

At this juncture, those of you familiar with spiritual direction may have your hands raised with the following objection: "This is sounding a lot like spiritual direction. Don't you think this is beyond the skill set of many in the parish, or even parish leaders?"

My answer: Perhaps. This type of interview may require a lot of subtlety, sensitivity, and spirituality – perhaps more than you think that you have. Be realistic about your personal gifts and talents! However, I think that, more often than not, we sell ourselves short in this arena. We don't expect the "Catholic-in-the-Pew" to be a person of prayer. We don't expect them to be able to ask the Holy Spirit for guidance in both emergency and everyday matters. We don't think that the average Catholic can say with any certainty, "I felt God's presence when..." In the same way we expect very little of ourselves. We relegate spirituality and discernment to mystics, monks and masters.

By all means, let people who are specially trained and prepared be spiritual directors, and refer your people to them for ongoing accompaniment and lifelong discernment. They would also be a great resource to train all who do volunteer interviews in the processing of discerning gifts for ministry. Think of this interview process as one very discreet moment along the journey, focused with laser-like precision on the relatively short term task of placing a willing volunteer into a ministry. Trust in what you know:

1. You know the ministry for which you are interviewing.

2. You know that the Holy Spirit has already been at work to bring this person to you. Don't second guess why this person came.

3. You know that by Baptism, the he or she has been called to ministry.

4. You know that they might very well have skills to do a formal parish ministry.

5. You know how to pray.

If these five things are not enough, then conduct your interview with another member of your team. Designate one person as the lead interviewer, but have the other person there mostly to listen. After the interview, pray with your discernment partner and discuss what you heard.

Never Try to Go It Alone

Another way to work this discernment is to leave your final decision about ministry candidates to a group of people. Have multiple staff members interview candidates, and then hold a discernment session with all interviewers. Pray together, and then invite each interviewer to report to the group on their conversation with a particular candidate, along with a recommendation. Be sure to invite the pastor parish administrator or another staff person to be part of this group, as they may know something critical about the person or situation. Make sure that everyone in the group offers feedback for each candidate, and then strive for 100 percent consensus on the final decision.

The outcome should be consensus on whether to place the candidate in a certain skilled or semi-skilled position, whether to do so with any stipulations, to recommend placement in another ministry, or to conclude that at this time the individual should not be invited into any ministry at all. The weightiness of the last option is often enough to encourage leaders to work with others on this discernment. It is all too easy to second guess yourself when you are making such a decision alone. It is also too easy for the pastor or another staff member to undermine your decision about the volunteer, if he or she has not been part of the discernment process all a

When You and Your Interviewee Don't Agree

In the best of cases, your potential volunteer is surprised by your discernment, but appreciative of the process. In the worst of cases, your potential volunteer becomes furious that he or she will not be able to do the ministry that he or she planned to do. This anger is only multiplied if the candidate feels that he or she has been called by God.

Jesus gave us an example of turning away someone who wanted to follow him. "As he [Jesus] was getting into the boat, the man who had been possessed [healed] pleaded to remain with him. But he would not permit him but told him instead, 'Go home to your family and announce to them all that the Lord in his pity has done for you.' Then the man went off and began to proclaim in the Decapolis what Jesus had done for him; and all were amazed." (Mark 5:18-19)

Many years ago my wife Laura had a volunteer come forward who wanted to teach the Bible. His zeal and interest were wonderful, but his knowledge of scripture was so limited that he would have done a great disservice to parishioners with his teaching. Laura informed him that before he could teach he would need to take a fair number of scripture courses offered by the diocese. After taking just a few courses, this man decided that teaching the Bible was not what he had thought it was, and he ended up in a different formal ministry.

This was a very difficult situation for my wife, because the man was insistent that God was calling him to teach the Bible. He complained to the pastor about her. However, Laura had already brought the pastor into the discernment process, and he both agreed with her assessment and backed her up when the man complained. Just the same, it took quite a bit of spunk to trust the discernment and hold firm.

Holding your ground in difficult situations will be easier if you have the following program elements in place:

1. Don't make any early promises. Never assume that someone is going to be placed in a ministry until the discernment is complete.

2. Transparency. The steps of the entire process, including the discernment, are clearly spelled out with the help of a flyer or brochure that interviewees receive early on in the process.

3. Invite the Spirit in. From the very start, encourage all potential volunteers to think of this as a discernment process – one that involves both them and the Church.

4. Get all key players on board. Make sure that all of the decision makers in the parish know how the discernment process works and support it.

5. Check your ego at the door. Keep reminding yourself that this is God's work, not yours.

6. Have a process of appeal and review. Spell out steps that you are willing to take if the potential volunteer asks you to reconsider. Consider when they might be able to reapply for the position, or what you might do to ensure that he or she has been heard.

Follow Your Joy

It is worthwhile to summarize this chapter by reiterating the advice I received from old Fr. Gareau so many years ago. As you help volunteers find a place of ministry in the Church, keep counsel of your own feelings. When a volunteer reaches a place of satisfaction and deep joy in his or her ministry, you will sense it, too. In the reverse fashion, you will sense when something is not quite right. Ask the Holy Spirit to help you find the way that leads to quiet assurance, even if it makes you anxious to tell someone something they don't want to hear.

Remember not to get too stuck at this point, because your adventure of learning and formation with your volunteers has just begun.

Chapter 7

Initial Formation, Jesus-Style

Make ministry formation part of the rhythm of your entire parish. Use global, focused and on-the-job formation to reach all levels of involvement. Use orientation, team meetings, mentors and more to give your volunteers initial training.

Leaders in both parish and diocesan ministry spend a lot of time wringing their hands over volunteer formation. They struggle with two conflicting questions: Have we have done enough to prepare volunteers for ministry? Will volunteers be scared away if we require more training? The Gospel portraits of Jesus provide a helpful vision for balancing these issues, particularly in the area of initial formation.

Jesus taught in the synagogues, on the streets, on the hillsides, and by the sea. He preached at great length to the crowds. As he spoke about the freedom of the Reign of God, he brought it to life by healing people of their infirmities, and setting them free from spiritual bondage. Anyone with an open heart and "ears that heard" (Matthew 13:16) had access to the message and could become part of the mission. Jesus called everyone and anyone to live their faith, to make faith come alive in the way that they loved God and neighbor. We can follow this global teaching strategy by providing ministry formation across all strata of parish life.

> **Jesus-Style Recruitment Tip #7: Train Along the Way**
>
> After crying out and convulsing him terribly, the unclean spirit came out, and the boy was like a corpse, so that most of them said, "He is dead." But Jesus took him by the hand and lifted him up, and he was able to stand. When he had entered the house, his disciples asked him privately, "Why could we not cast it out?" He said to them, "This kind can come out only through prayer." - Mark 9:26-29

As he proclaimed portions of the message to all people, Jesus also reserved many elements of teaching for his very closest companions. After presenting the Parable of the Sower to the crowds, he explained the parable in detail to his disciples (Matthew 13:10); to his disciples alone he revealed the true nature of his mission (Mark 9:31); only with his closest friends did he share the gift of the Eucharist (Luke 22:19), strategies for evangelizing (Matthew 10), the agony of Gethsemane (March 14:32ff), and the breath of his Peace (John 14:27). In a similar manner, our initial training of volunteers will offer more information to those who will perform more demanding tasks.

True Jesus-Style formation requires both of these aspects; we need to train globally and individually. There is nothing revolutionary in that. However, adding a third Jesus-Style method to the mix offers fresh perspective.

Time and time again, Jesus was a minister of the moment. He did not teach from a fixed curriculum presented over the course of an orderly symposium, but from the fluid and ever-changing curriculum of everyday life. He used spontaneous moments like the question about paying tax to the emperor (Matthew 22:16ff), the storm at sea (Mark 4:35ff), and picking wheat on the Sabbath (Luke 6:1) to teach his disciples about the role of faith in their everyday lives. In moments like healing of a leper (Mark 1:41), responding to the faith of a Canaanite woman (Matthew 15:22-28), and conversation with the woman of Samaria (John 4), he showed them how to minister beyond their comfort zone to the outcast and foreigner. He invited disciples with little or no knowledge of the Reign of God to "come and see" what it was all about (John 1:39). Jesus' followers learn by observing him. However, they did not fully understand the import of his teachings and actions until much later, after he had revealed his resurrected glory to them.

Defer to your (arch)diocesan offices for required and ongoing volunteer training. At the same time, use these three methods of Jesus as your guide for providing initial, parish-based formation for your volunteers:

1. *Global formation* about ministry for the entire parish

2. *Focused formation* for those who are doing the ministries

3. *On-the-job formation* and for semi-skilled and skilled volunteers.

You are likely already doing work in all three of these areas. As we consider each of these aspects, see if a deliberate, Jesus-Style focus changes your feelings about formation, or suggests new disciple-building strategies.

Global Formation

Does your parish have a ministry mindset? Do you have the explicit goal of activating every single member to live their baptismal call? Does every baptized member know that they have been commissioned priest, prophet and king? Do you have an intentional strategy to make this happen? Let us examine three tools that we use to reach out to the entire parish, with an eye for ministry formation.

1. The Parish Bulletin

When it comes to the bulletin, most parishes make two faulty assumptions. First, they assume that everyone who receives a bulletin reads the bulletin. Second, they assume that they can get people to read items simply by announcing them. There is little that we can do here about the first assumption. Many parishes would do well to think about their bulletin as a newsletter, and present their features and articles in a more engaging way. That is another discussion, for another time! However, if you want to use your bulletin successfully to promote parish ministries, we must closely examine the second assumption. Does this notice look familiar?

ST. BALLYHOO OUTREACH COMMITTEE

The St. Ballyhoo Parish Outreach Committee brings the Spiritual and Corporal Works of Mercy to life for needy people in the parish and our greater community. Volunteers visit the homebound, make baby blankets for our Elizabeth Ministry, help with our food drives, pack "Thanks-in-Giving" holiday meals for the needy,. We bring the concern and love of the parish to those whom we do not immediately see around the Table of the Lord. Some training required. If you are interested in becoming part of this important ministry, call Jane Doe at 555-5555.

There is no doubt that you could get some responses to this ad. It has happened enough to make us think this is an acceptable way to publish. However, you will have a much better chance of getting people to read and respond to it if you focus not on describing the tasks, but clearly showing them the *personal benefits* of volunteering. As I mentioned in Chapter 5, the most effective way to do this is to include testimonials.

On a regular basis, my home parish spotlights one of the ministry areas with a full page bulletin insert. The article always includes conversation with people who are doing the ministry. Use a similar method to systematically promote the ministries in the parish. Think of this as an "up-close-and-personal-with" type of article. Include a photo of the volunteer or volunteers you want to spotlight. Interview them with questions like the following:

"How did you get involved in this ministry?"

"Can you describe a moment that made you feel happy to be a volunteer in one of our parish ministries?"

"What advice do you have for someone considering volunteering?"

Let the personal story carry the article. Include some interesting, little-known facts about the volunteers themselves, or the people they serve. To guide your writing, ask yourself, "What would catch my eye to read this article?" and "Where are we including both the personal challenges and benefits of volunteering?" With your parish leadership, plan a systematic campaign for these articles. When you are doing the recruiting campaign described earlier, focus all of your articles on the ministry area for which you are recruiting. Use the rest of the assigned inserts—whether you do them every other week, monthly, or at some other interval—to highlight other ministries.

Including this type of human interest feature on a regular basic will not only spread the word about your ministries, but may also have the secondary benefit of encouraging more of your parishioners to read the bulletin.

2. The Parish Mission Statement

Does your parish mission statement that concisely and vividly capture the ministerial spirit of the parish community? If not, get one, and use it. The last parish where I worshiped printed their mission statement in the Sunday bulletin and inserted it in their hymnal. The parish has children memorize it, and the pastor mentions it several times throughout the year, particularly during Lent and Advent. It is a statement that unequivocally steers everything they do. If you don't know where to find your parish mission statement, or even if you have one, inquire about it. Often with change of pastors and staff the mission statement does not get reviewed or is buried in some committee's to-do list.

3. The Homily

As a pivotal moment in the Sunday celebration of the Eucharist, the homily is a natural place to provide global ministry formation. However, at first blush it appears that there are way too many other special occasions or moments demanding homily time. Parishes observe Catholic School Week, Vocations Awareness Week, Scout Sunday, Catechetical Sunday, and Mission Sunday. There are evangelization campaigns, stewardship campaigns, diocesan collection campaigns, building campaigns, and, of course, the recruitment campaign described earlier in this book. If campaigns aren't enough, there are celebrations of Baptism, First Eucharist, Confirmation, and more. In short, there are very few weekends without some special homily cause or theme. With all of these occasions demanding homiletic attention or mention, what can preachers do to bring ministry formation into the mix on any sort of regular basis?

In my view there is plenty they can do. Not only that, but there is likely a lot of ministry formation already happening in the Sunday homily. With just small amounts of focus and planning, you can compound your effectiveness.

If Jesus-Style Recruitment is about forming disciples to serve the Reign of God, then most preachers are already doing it. Around the country preachers of the Word regularly encourage parishioners to put their baptismal call into action. Every time the Gospel is proclaimed, Jesus Christ breaks into the assembly. When priests or deacons help us to connect Christ's story with ours, we hear the same message that throngs by the Sea of Galilee, in the streets of Jerusalem, or on the road to Emmaus heard from the mouth of Jesus himself. Any time that a homilist is truly preaching a homily, he is teaching his parish how to minister as a disciple.

The only thing that we need to add to these efforts is intention and organization. You can do this with the two previous global tools: add intention to your homilies by incorporating your parish mission statement, and organize your homilies with the structure you establish for your parish bulletin campaign.

In the marketing and PR world today, there is a lot of buzz about "branding." Among other things, this method includes consistently presenting your preferred image of your company to the public. You use logos, slogans, and other themes to project a strong message to the public. Your parish mission statement conveys this same type of "branded" message. You spell out to people clearly and succinctly what you are about as a parish. After enough times of hearing it, they begin to "get" it and take pride in it.

Taking regular opportunities throughout the year to connect your homily with the parish mission statement, and people will begin to articulate and tell others who you are as a parish, and what the parishes priorities are. They will begin to understand that they are part of a community that does not just talk about faith, but puts it in action.

The organizing portion of this is almost as simple as the intention part. Once you set up a schedule for the bulletin articles and interviews described above, it will be easy enough to mention the ministry or even use the lived example of the people mentioned in the homily. This part of the homily need not take up your entire time. It should be easy to connect whatever Gospel story you have on a given week with a parishioner's acts of kindness, mercy, compassion and love.

With a relatively small amount of effort, you can use the three elements of the parish *bulletin*, a parish *mission statement*, and the *homily* to provide remarkably extensive formation to a large segment of your parish.

Focused Formation

In the same manner that Jesus demanded much more of those who were his closest companions, we should demand more of those who are most deeply committed to the mission of the parish. What is a reasonable amount of initial formation? The following outline should provide a solid point of reference.

1. Formation Activities for All Volunteers

Everyone who is volunteering in your parish should receive some orientation to ministry. This orientation should include an outline of the vision for that particular ministry, and then a broad view of how all of the ministries within a given area serve the greater purpose of the parish. You will accomplish this end handily if the ministry recruitment campaign described early runs as expected, "by the book;" the Ministry Orientation meetings I have described can do this. However, there are very few things in the parish that end up running by the book! It may not be feasible to get all Level 1 and Level 2 volunteers to an orientation meeting. In that case, you will have to resort to providing written materials, or maybe even an online orientation.

I have already suggested that you focus your recruitment campaigns on one ministry area at a time. This might convey the impression that you should only hold orientations for one ministry each year. This is by no means the case! Even if you focus major recruitment on just one area, every ministry area will have new volunteers yearly. Therefore, every ministry area will have to provide orientation, every year. However, you need not run four, five, six, seven separate orientations, by ministry topic. Design a single ministry orientation for all volunteers, and allow extra time for participants to break out into the various ministry areas to discuss specifics (SEE APPENDIX).

This orientation should accomplish two things for your Level 1, 2 and 3 volunteers:

1. It should inspire them with the importance of their contribution to the mission of the parish.

2. It should present them with a clear picture of the deeper ways that they might get involved with the ministries of the parish.

The same inspiration that Providers, Helpers, and Professional Career Volunteers receive will give Skilled and Semi-skilled Volunteers the motivation that they will need to go even further with training.

2. Formation for Professional Career Volunteers

Level 3 volunteers bring the expertise of their chosen field to the parish. They have already established skills and ongoing education. Whether they are medical workers, plumbers, carpenters, professional actors, artists, nuclear physicists, professional athletes, auto mechanics, forest rangers, quilters, or entertainers, they already know their craft. The way that they *apply* their skills in the parish will determine the additional formation that they need.

If they are simply acting as consultants for a project or offering their services for free or at a reduced rate, they will need little or no additional training. If they will have significant interaction with other parishioners or apply their skills in a unique way to parish life, they will need a lot more. For instance, a drama teacher who is working with Confirmation candidates to develop skits on the Gifts of the Holy Spirit will need an overview of the Confirmation program itself, and perhaps even skills for leading faith sharing with youth. A contractor who is directing a parish building project for the homeless may need a deeper understanding of Catholic social teaching, or the Church's preferential option for the poor. Any activity involving substantial contact with the children will require child protect training from the (arch)diocese. Consider each Professional Career Volunteer individually, as each person's background, even within the same field or specialty, can be decidedly different.

3. Formation for Skilled and Semi-Skilled Volunteers

Level 4 and 5 volunteers will require the most formation. In most cases, these will be the volunteers you will send for extended (arch)diocesan formation programs. Since the distinctions between these two levels are variable, it will be best to consider them together.

Beyond the broad orientation that all volunteers receive, what do these volunteers need? To get them started in ministry, you will need to provide both basic training and ongoing formation.

Basic Training

I will not spend a lot of time here, because most parishes already provide this type of training. You give volunteers the "survival skills" that they need to perform the ministry. This includes procedures, policies, and basic job requirements. If you do this well, you show them how others who are the most successful in the ministry do it. You work them through the basic elements of the ministry, and then give them a chance to practice or review necessary skills. This "boot camp" is usually short and intense—as short as two hours to as long as ten or twenty.

Your volunteers leave this training knowing what they have to do, where and when they do it, and perhaps even something of how to do it. However, most of the "how" comes only with further training. If you have done this basic training well, your volunteers will be grateful for all that they have learned, but also concerned that perhaps they need more to be effective.

Ongoing Formation

Parish leaders fret over the time required for ongoing formation. They ask questions like: "With all that I am asking my volunteers to do already, how can I possibly ask them to go to training?" "I feel overwhelmed at times. How can I fit formation into the already crowded parish calendar?"

> **Do not build formation ONTO what you do, but rather INTO what you do.**

While both of these questions appear to raise very practical concerns, I believe that is more about attitude than practice. If you believe deep down that ministry formation is first and foremost about forming disciples, then stand firm in your belief that you are offering your volunteers an indescribable gift. At the same time, you must rigorously ask yourself if the formation they take part in is indeed a gift for them. Is it substantial, and of high quality? Does it inspire them? Does it inspire you? Does it not just provide skills, but also make them better Christians, better adults?

My second response is imminently practical. Do not build formation ONTO what you do, but rather INTO what you do. Here are some examples:

In-services and Team Meetings

Schedule your own or even diocesan training during a time when your volunteers would regularly meet. For catechists of all ages, offer quarterly sessions during their regularly scheduled class time, and provide childcare for those who normally bring their children with them. For liturgical ministers, offer the sessions on Sunday between or after the masses. For those who simply hold monthly meetings, pick a month once a year where you will provide updating and formation rather than the normal agenda. Better yet, incorporate fifteen to twenty minutes of formation into the agenda every time you meet! Distribute a helpful article to all volunteers ahead of time, and plan a shared discussion at your regular meeting.

My mind goes immediately to the 80's TV series "Hill Street Blues." Almost every episode began with all of the police offers in the morning briefing, getting the update on the day's crime scene and assignments. Often it ended with the Chief's admonition, "Be careful. It's a jungle out there." Depending upon the ministry, you might find such a gathering—even one as short as ten minutes—helpful. Don't underestimate the formation and community building that can happen in a very concentrated but well planned time.

Mentoring

Mentoring, or the pairing of veterans with newcomers, takes place not just in church ministry, but across countless professions and trades. The idea is as old as the apprentice who learned his trade under the master craftsman. If you want to go back even earlier, it is obviously the model practiced by an Itinerant Rabbi and his eager Disciples.

Make this model your hinge pin for ministry formation. Pair every newbie with a veteran. For that matter, pair every existing volunteer with another. Set up a period during which the newcomer must shadow the veteran, and provide discussion aides to help the mentor and mentee talk about what they heard and saw while performing the ministry. In this relationship, the newcomer picks up invaluable hints and ideas about how to do the ministry. He or she has a person with whom to share the joys and struggles. The veteran receives the gift of knowing they are helping another. Not only that, but the energy, enthusiasm, and occasional trepidation of the newcomer can recharge the veteran's batteries and help him or her to reconnect with his or her original zeal for ministry. This is a win-win-win: Both newcomer and veteran win, and you win some amazing formation with little to no effort on your part.

The 60 Second Check-In

One day while serving in my second year as a parish catechetical leader, I was sitting at my disk reading catechist evaluations. On the form I had asked them to offer some comments about how their year went, and whether they were planning to return the following year. I stopped short as I read the evaluation of one of the catechists. She informed me that no, she was not coming back next year, and that her class that year had been horrible. She would never put herself through that torture again. As you can imagine, I felt horrible as well. Not only was it news to me that she wasn't returning, I had no idea that her experience had been so devastating. I had dealt with occasional discipline problems in the class, but she had never approached me with her struggles and anxieties.

I vowed to myself that I would never be so "out of the loop" again! The solution: The 60 Second Check-In. I made sure that every time my volunteers met, I touched based with every one of them for at least 60 seconds. It was easy to do. I stopped in the classroom anytime throughout our gatherings, or I even stood and listened outside in the hall of a group that had problems the previous week. As catechists left, I asked them how it went, and if they needed anything from me. Often the responses were routine, but I also often caught wind of an issue that needed my attention, or a resource that I could provide.

If your ministry doesn't take place on the parish property, then the 60 Second Check-In is a bit harder to do. Catch your volunteers coming and going from Sunday Mass, or perhaps you will have to resort to making phone calls. You will likely have to leave a voice message like: "Hey, Charles, this is Chris. Just touching base. How are things going with your home visits? Thanks so much for the email update on Mrs. Jones. We did not know that her husband was in the hospital, and we will be sure a staff member goes to see him. Can I help you with anything? I hope to see you at the team meeting on Sunday, but please feel free to call me or email me if you need anything at all."

Often this simple communication technique can evolve into a "teachable moment" that helps your volunteer become better equipped for ministry. Use it to maximum effect every week.

Diocesan Formation

Just about any parish can use the above activities to form volunteers. When it comes to more intense and substantial training, though, we often run out of gas. Most dioceses and archdioceses stand ready and willing to help. Build time into your schedules to encourage your volunteers to take part in this training.

Chapter 8

Less Thanks, More Constructive Praise

Remember that you have recruited volunteers not to be thanked, but to serve. Instead of going overboard with elaborate appreciation initiatives, perks, or compensation, focus on consistent, constructive praise. The results may surprise you.

Jesus-Style Recruiting has very dramatic implications for what we have traditionally called "volunteer appreciation." I believe that we need to radically rethink this component of our parish programming.

Conventional wisdom suggests that, for all they do as volunteers, we cannot thank them enough. The sky is the limit when we come to volunteer appreciation. Neighboring parishes attempt to outdo one another with elaborate end of year parties, incentives, and even award ceremonies. There seems to be an implicit assumption here that showing our volunteers that we are really, really grateful for what they do is a major component of keeping them on the job.

The more I reflect upon Jesus-Style Ministry, the more I am convinced that we have gotten off the mark with appreciation. Now, I am not the Ebenezer Scrooge of thank-you dinners and recognition ceremonies. After all, such occasions build rapport and community among volunteers, and offer moments to promote the value of the ministry. I have served in enough volunteer situations to feel both the warmth of a "thank you" and the unpleasant feeling of being taken for granted. There is nothing wrong with gratitude! However, this book's lengthy consideration of volunteer ministry as discipleship should give us pause, and even suggest other methods that may bear better fruit.

> **Jesus-Style Recruitment**
> **Tip #8: Let the Kingdom be its own reward.**
>
> Jesus replied, "Who among you would say to your slave who has just come in from plowing or tending sheep in the field, 'Come here at once and take your place at the table'? Would you not rather say to him, 'Prepare supper for me, put on your apron and serve me while I eat and drink; later you may eat and drink'? Do you thank the slave for doing what was commanded? So you also, when you have done all that you were ordered to do, say, 'We are worthless slaves; we have done only what we ought to have done!'" - Luke 17:7–10

Reflect upon your own walk of ministry. Do you do it for the thanks? Do you do it in order to be appreciated? I am betting that you don't. The portion of our ministry that we perform as ministry (apart from the portion that puts bread on the table) we do because we have been drawn into it. We do it because it has felt "right" for our lives; we do it because God called us to do it. Sometimes gratitude gives us a boost when we serve, but most of the time, what keeps us going is knowing that we are the right person, in the right place, doing the right thing. We do it because it suits us; we are called to do it. After the Bread of Life discourse, many would-be followers of Jesus leave in dismay. When Jesus asks his disciples if they, too, will leave, Simon Peter says, "Lord, to whom can we go? You have the words of eternal life." (John 6:68)

They stay because they must, because it is the only thing that suits their life. When we are doing true discipleship-ministry, that is why we stay, too.

Consider again the gift of ministry. The Kingdom of God is its own reward. If we believe this to be true, and if we deeply believe that drawing volunteers into ministry is a priceless gift for their lives, then thanking them is not the huge priority that conventional wisdom proclaims it to be. Appreciation is not, and should not be, our prime motivator.

> **To keep volunteers motivated in ministry, we need to help them understand that they are doing something God wants them to do.**

What then, is the prime motivator? We do not need to talk ourselves giddy to discover it. It is, as we have already said, the Kingdom of God. To keep volunteers motivated in ministry, we need to help them understand that they are doing something God wants them to do. We need to help them see that the Kingdom of God is made real through their actions, through their words, through their ministry.

We can do this through constructive praise. Instead of simply thanking your volunteers for what they do, take note of what they are doing well, and praise them for it. Give them a clear idea of how their actions contribute to the greater welfare of the parish, and build up the Body of Christ. Constructive praise is a lot harder than simply saying thank you, but is much more likely to reap significant results. The way to do this is twofold:

1. Be Specific.

If are vague and general in your praise, volunteers will wonder if you really mean it. Give a direct example of what your volunteer has done, and tell them why you think this action merits your praise.

Instead of just saying: "Nice job on the retreat team last week, Jane," say "You were a great help on the retreat team last week, Jane. I appreciated the way that you actively listened to the teenagers in your small group, and got everyone to participate. You even drew John into the discussions. He is so reserved! He had a great retreat due in large part to how you helped him come out of his shell."

Specific praise not only makes people feel good about what they did; it also encourages them to continue the positive behavior and apply it to the rest of their volunteer experience.

2. Connect It with Discipleship.

Bring it all back to the Reign of God. Make a direct connection between the great action that the volunteer performed, and the greater purpose of the ministry. Continuing with the previous example, you might add the following:

"Jane, focusing on your entire group, and giving them each a chance to participate, modeled the ministry of Christ for them. I am sure that it was a lot easier for them to catch the theme of our retreat, 'Following Jesus,' when they experienced such acceptance in their small group."

This is constructive praise because it not only builds up your volunteer, but it also builds up their knowledge of the greater purpose, and advances the mission of your parish. Use this concept to "makeover" the ways that you are accustomed to saying thank you. Here are a few ideas:

From Thank You Notes to Praise Notes

With just a little more effort, supercharge your practice of writing thank you notes to volunteers. Make it your daily mission to catch your volunteers doing a great job. Create a log containing the names of all your volunteers, and set aside time in your schedule every week to observe them in action. Notice when your lector proclaims the Word particularly well, when a parishioner calls the office just to say how much they appreciated your home visitor's assistance, when you overhear your catechist responding particularly well to a learner's question. Note the accomplishment in your log. Send the volunteer a notecard (yes, a notecard, and not an email) with specific details about what they did well. If appropriate, add suggestions for follow up, or refer to resources that he or she may find helpful.

Observation and Feedback

You can incorporate these same moments of observation into a more formal process. Leave space in your log to make notes about skills that the volunteer needs to refine, or other ways in which they might improve. Another way to do this is to complete a formal observation summary. See the sample at the end of this chapter. In the summary reiterate what the volunteer did well. Note his or her shortcomings as well, and areas where he or she needs to grow.

Set up a time to review the formal observation with your volunteer. The easiest way to do this is to catch a few minutes with them before or after the next time they perform their ministry. Reiterate the positive first, and frame any areas for improvement as opportunities for them to be more effective in their ministry. Once again, it is best to keep this review fairly short, in proportion to the skills and depth of commitment required. Unless your observation uncovered serious deficiencies to make you question whether the volunteer should continue in ministry, it should be a boost of encouragement for the volunteer, and an opportunity for you to reinforce your support for him or her.

Use the log to work systematically through your entire list of volunteers. It doesn't matter how long it takes to get through your list. It just matters that you develop the habit of constructive praise. If you frame it positively, your volunteers will accept even criticism as a means to helping them grow as disciples.

Stipends and Other Incentives

This is another area where I fear we run the risk of overdoing it. Many catechetical leaders offer reduced or free tuition for children if a parent volunteers as a catechist in the program. Some even pay their volunteers a small stipend. I am not in favor of the latter; I believe that stipends send mixed signals to volunteers. A paid volunteer is no longer a volunteer, even if the pay is not close to a living wage. This establishes an entirely different set of expectations between parish and parishioner. The volunteer's service is no longer "priceless," but has a fixed price, and the volunteer "owes" the parish his or her service. Eventually, the size of the stipend will lead the volunteer to scale back his or her involvement, resulting in exactly the opposite effect as the one intended.

Other perks like reduced tuition, paid training programs, and occasional luncheons or outings, are different. They can build camaraderie among volunteers, and give them a deeper sense of belonging. This reminds me of giving blood. I am a frequent donor, and often participate in a drive where they give away a free t-shirt. Not only that, but they always have nice cookies in the snack area afterwards! I do not give blood for these benefits, but it makes my experience more enjoyable. The Red Cross might spend as much $1.00 to $2.00 per person to provide refreshments and small gifts at blood drives. This is acceptable hospitality. However, everyone would start to get concerned if the Red Cross offered even $1.00 in cash to everyone who gave blood. Why would that idea disturb donors? The reason is that suddenly we have fixed a price on something that should simply remain priceless.

In this area, the "makeover" is a matter of emphasis. By all means, nurture your volunteers. Provide nice food for meetings, and throw the occasional community-building event for them. But be careful not to cheapen their service by giving any type of impression that you are attaching a price tag to it. If you offer free or reduced tuition to certain volunteers fight against the urge to make this a strong part of your "sell" for the ministry. Focus instead on the benefits of serving as a disciple. Let the Kingdom be its own reward.

The End of the Year Celebration

My problem with large volunteer appreciation events is not so much that we should stop thanking people for volunteering. It is more practical than that. Jesus-Style Recruiting centers on the idea that everyone is called to live out their baptismal call in being Christ for others. Your goal as a Jesus-Style Recruiter is to activate your entire parish for ministry. If you successfully level your ministries your ranks will swell with people with all levels of commitment. Your largest groups of volunteers could well be Level 1, 2, and 3 volunteers. Not only that, but your message will have gone out to hundreds of parishioners who are not working in any church ministry, but are proclaiming the Gospel in the marketplace of their everyday lives.

If this is true, whom should you invite to the big party? Just the semi-skilled and skilled volunteers? Just those people who are putting in some magical number of hours? No. If ministry is the entire parish's business, then you should invite the entire parish to the party. Anything short of a global invitation runs the risk of leaving someone out. Not only that, but it sends a very distinct message that only an elite few minister in the parish. Follow this train of thought to its logical conclusion: Is there not a danger that end of the year appreciation events actually run counter to your intended purpose, and discourage people from volunteering? We always complain about having the "same old people" doing all of the volunteering in the parish. Doesn't the ministry appreciation event perpetuate this problem?

Despite these potential flaws, I do not think we need to abandon large scale ministry appreciation events. As with other appreciation initiatives, I would like to propose a "makeover" idea to bring a Jesus-Style perspective.

Apply the components of constructive praise. How can we be both specific and discipleship-centered in our praise without singling out select groups of volunteers? The simplest way to accomplish this is to focus not on people on ministry.

Instead of naming volunteers, name the ministries that happened in the past year. Can you give your parishioners a sense of the enormity and breadth of the parish's outreach? Work through your entire list of volunteer ministries, and come up with ways to quantify them; add up, or at least estimate, the intentions collected by your parishioners praying at home, the number of shut ins visited, the hours your catechists logged, the blood pressures taken by your parish nurses, the songs sung at mass by pastoral musicians, the dozens of baked goods donated for various occasions. Draw your parish ministry leaders into this exercise. I bet you will find some amazing data from all levels of ministry.

After you have quantified the ministries about which you have some knowledge, consider some of the anonymous things that your parishioners did out in the world. How many spoke kindly to the discouraged person at work, the post office, grocery store, or bank? How many said a prayer for someone whom they were having trouble forgiving? How many were honest when it would have been much more convenient to lie, or patient when it would have been easier to fly off the handle? The data you will propose here is nebulous, in the realm of "what-ifs", but the potential Gospel incidents applied to your congregation could number in the thousands. These moments are beautiful; find a way to remind your parishioners that they experience them.

What is the best way to recognize these accomplishments? Bring them to a parish-wide event, like the annual picnic. Take five or ten minutes for this litany of ministry, perhaps interspersed with refrains of "We thank you, Lord" at an extended blessing before the meal. Be sure to link this litany with your parish mission statement and the baptismal call to discipleship. It could be as simple as that. You could also use this litany in your parish recruitment campaign.

Commissioning of Ministers

We must take a few words to consider special commissioning ceremonies. Most parishes commission any number of volunteers, from pastoral council members, to extraordinary ministers of the Eucharist, to catechists. Where do these functions fit within a Jesus-Style Recruiting perspective?

I am sure it is obvious by now that I would frown upon commissioning services that promote any type of elitism among volunteers. If you are doing these services simply as a form of special recognition, stop and reconsider them for reasons stated in the previous section. Gratuitously elevating one ministry over others will discourage the others. At the same time, there are perfectly acceptable times and ways to use commissioning ceremonies.

Take commissioning of your pastoral council as an example. The people chosen for this ministry serve on behalf of the entire community. It is only fitting that they be publicly delegated to perform this work. Their volunteer ministry is the whole parish's ministry. As we all pray for the success of their work, we pray for the work of the parish to move forward, and we recognize that through them, we all have a hand in what the parish does.

Catechetical Sunday is a day of special observance in the churches of the United States, where parishes are encouraged to promote and celebrate the Church's teaching ministry. I have heard a number of pastors rule against commissioning catechists on this day, with the argument that if we commission catechists then we should commission all of the volunteers in the parish, because there are a lot of other people putting in long hours of service for the Church. I cannot wholly disagree with this argument, for the very reasons outlined earlier in this chapter; we should heed the warning to avoid elitism. At the same time, catechesis has taken center stage in the Church's priorities for this age. The Church has devoted millions and millions of dollars, and countless resource hours to forming disciples in parishes and Catholic schools. Authentically handing on the faith to the next generation is arguably the task for the Church of this generation. If this is true, then it makes sense to shine a special spotlight on this ministry. Catechetical commissioning ceremonies can make that happen.

In keeping with Jesus-Style Ministry, make the focus of commissioning ceremonies not the ministers, but the ministry. When I worked in a parish I wrote a Catechetical Sunday ceremony that commissioned catechists and parish leaders first, but then invited parents to stand to be commissioned. We invited them to be the first teachers of their children, to catechize by both word and example, and they responded, "We will." Then we invited the children to stand, to dedicate themselves to sharing the Good News on the playground, at home, and wherever they went. They, too, responded, "We will." Finally we invited the whole parish to stand, and exhorted everyone to be Christ to others and to echo the Word of God in all they did. As we all stood together and said, "We will," I felt the satisfaction that we were truly commissioning Jesus-Style.

Rome (or any place) Wasn't Built in a Day...

Of all the ideas I have proposed so far, I wonder if this chapter poses the greatest challenge. Parish leaders feel deeply indebted to their volunteers. They know all too well that volunteers are the lifeblood coursing through a parish's veins, keeping its heart beating. At this point, it may be too much for you to rethink the way that you do volunteer appreciation. If that is the case, let me reassure you that this is the eighth chapter for a reason; there are plenty of other aspects of Jesus-Style Recruiting to consider before getting to this one.

Chapter 9
Let Them Go

Use this simple process for re-signing volunteers every year. Here's why it works, and how it will build your program rather than deplete it.

The idea for this chapter came from an experience I had at my last parish, St. Katharine Drexel, in Frederick, MD. I mention the parish and the pastor, Fr. Keith Boisvert, by name, because the practice I am about to describe was his creation. The idea is simple, but elegant, and ties in perfectly with Jesus-Style Recruitment.

I volunteered as coordinator of the liturgy planning committee in the parish. I worked in that capacity for several years. I enjoyed both the work and the people with whom I volunteered, but a significant reason why I did it so long was because I was set free every year. Fr. Keith sends a letter to all ministry leaders every year, thanking them for their service, and inviting them to a special dinner. He tells them that he does not want to take the immense gift of their time and talent for granted, and asks them to prayerfully consider if they want to continue in the ministry for another year. He also gives them an opportunity to recommend another person whom they think might be a good person to lead the ministry in the coming year. That's about all there is to it. See a sample of Fr. Keith's letter at the end of the chapter.

> **Jesus-Style Recruiting Tip #9:**
> **Let them go.**
>
> Jesus unrolled the scroll and found the place where it was written: "The Spirit of the Lord is upon me, because he has anointed me to bring good news to the poor. He has sent me to proclaim release to the captives and recovery of sight to the blind, to let the oppressed go free, to proclaim the year of the Lord's favor." Luke 4:17-19

Some people might deem it risky business to send such a letter to all of your ministry leaders every year. What if they all throw in the towel at once? For goodness' sake, he shouldn't plant the idea of leaving in their heads, should he? Is it a trick, some kind of sneaky reverse psychology scheme? I don't know about that, but I do know a couple of things:

    1) It worked on me and

    2) It definitely catches the spirit of Jesus-Style Ministry.

For Fr. Keith there is a very practical benefit for the parish in this process. Inviting ministry leaders to reconsider their roles each year encourages them to perform their ministry joyfully. Fr. Keith explained it to me this way:

"People sometimes feel 'trapped' in a position they have held for a while, but don'tknow how to resign. Sometimes they feel guilty resigning. When people feel trapped, they become resentful and don't do a good job—not a good attitude for someone in ministry. So, our ministry leaders have the opportunity and the freedom every year to reaffirm their desire to continue in that leadership position.

And when they decide to move on, we have the opportunity at the dinner to thank them for their service, and even welcome the new leader aboard." This was my personal experience. It was refreshing to have a new start at the ministry each year, to be given the freedom to stop and discern whether it was still the right thing to do. Rather than feeling tempted to quit each year, I felt valued and respected, and happy to freely rejoin the cause. Knowing that I wasn't trapped in the ministry for the rest of my life made this something that I did joyfully.

As a matter of fact, when I did finally leave, it took me two years to decide. I left with a feeling of peaceful satisfaction, instead of that wasted, burned out surliness that volunteers can have when they stay at it too long.

Doesn't this process emulate the way that Jesus interacted with people? His proclamation of the Kingdom always called people to freedom. Every act of healing, every act of compassion and every moment of forgiveness that he created was to set people's spirits free. His final act of love on the Cross set us free from the chains of death. His Resurrection drove that point home. Talk about setting the bar for ministry. Can we do anything less than to make sure that we lead those within our charge to deep and lasting freedom?

Contrary to what you might expect, this process does not encourage a mass exodus of volunteers every year. Take this past year as an example. Of the approximately fifty volunteers who serve as ministry leaders in Fr. Keith's parish, only two leaders stepped down this past year. Both of them had been serving six to eight years in their positions.

Set Your Volunteers Free.

Jesus-Style Recruiting calls us to adapt Fr. Keith's method to our work with volunteers. What would it look like if we set not just our ministry leaders, but ALL OF OUR VOLUNTEERS FREE, every year?

When I was a parish catechetical leader, I sent out renewal forms every year to my catechists. However, it was just my catechists, my skilled volunteers, whom I invited to discern their commitment for the coming year. I never included the other four levels of ministry. As I think about it, I more or less took their continued ministry for granted. I also did not ask my catechists to name someone suitable to take their place should they decide to leave. As a matter of fact, I stepped very lightly on the discernment aspect, hoping that my catechists would simply renew without thinking. Had I been more keenly focused on Jesus-Style ministry, I might have taken a different path.

At first blush, it looks like a logistical nightmare to send ministry renewal forms to every volunteer. If we are effective in recruitment, this could mean letters to hundreds and hundreds of parishioners. How many hours will it take to sort this task out? How many trees will have to be pulped for the tons of paperwork required?

Let me agree at the outset that setting your volunteers free each year will require effort. I will take it one step further to say that, wherever possible, you should work this process in person. While you might send initial information out via letter or email, it would be best to formalize the volunteer's decision with a meeting. As I have stated in previous chapters, there is no satisfactory substitute for the face-to-face meeting. There is no better way to convey your care and respect for the volunteer. There is no better way to help them connect this discernment with their journey of Christian discipleship.

While personal contact is critical, there is no reason why one or two people have to make all of the contacts. Seasoned leaders, who supervise the various ministers, could take charge of this function. Just make sure that they fully understand the rationale behind the process, and can convey the message well. A walk through the steps might best illustrate what I mean.

   1. Send a letter.

The initial letter need not be long, and an email might do the trick. With a word of thanks, invite the volunteer into discernment for the following year. Write something like this:

> Dear _____:
>
> As you complete a year of ministry as _____, I give thanks to God for the way in which your service has built up the Body of Christ. I invite you to pause and reflect on this past year, and to prayerfully consider whether you would like to continue in this volunteer ministry another year.
>
> We ask you to renew your commitment every year, because we do not want to take your service for granted. We also know that you will be more effective in ministry if you freely and joyfully make it part of your life. Over the next few weeks, I will be setting up appointments to speak about this with all of our volunteers. Can you respond to this note with a time that is good for us to speak in person, or on the phone for a few minutes?
>
> In the meantime, the following questions might be helpful as you reflect and pray:
>
> 1. How have I experienced Christ in a deeper way through my service to the parish this year?
>
> 2. What have been the rewards of volunteering? What have been the challenges?
>
> 3. Is the Lord calling me to continue in this ministry? Or do I sense that I can better serve him in a different way?
>
> 4. Does anyone else come to mind whom we should invite to join us in this ministry?
>
> I look forward to speaking with you!
>
> Sincerely,

2. Meet to discuss.

When I say "meet" here, I am not suggesting a lengthy sit-down. As a matter of fact, five to ten minutes is plenty of time. Meet them after or before mass, or plan it around a time when the volunteer is already at the parish.

I have left out a step titled "set up the meeting time" because, in many cases, this meeting will happen over the phone when you call to set up a meeting. This will work fine for a volunteer whom you know pretty well. However, if the individual is less familiar to you, it would be best to meet face-to-face.

Open with a quick prayer to the Holy Spirit. Reiterate the purpose of the gathering, and invite them to share responses to the questions you posed in your letter. Take notes if necessary, but be sure to actively listen to what your interviewee is saying. By his or her tone of voice, energy level, and body language, you should get an instant sense of how he or she feels about the past year.

3. Invite them back.

Remind them that in your original note you asked them to prayerfully consider whether or not they would continue in that ministry for the coming year. Then, ask them outright. Again listen carefully to their response. Respect their answer, whether it be "yes," or "no," or "I have to think about it some more." It is okay to ask for clarification of their reason if they say they are not returning. Perhaps a situation has changed at home, or they feel called to minister in another area. Perhaps they can identify no reason at all, except that it feels like it is time to quit. Assume that the Holy Spirit is at work in whatever answer you hear.

4. Pray a prayer of gratitude.

No matter how they respond to the invitation, ask if there is any way that you can be helpful to them. Perhaps they need more information about other parish ministries, or additional resources for discernment. If they need more time to think about it, set a tentative date to meet again. Stand confident in your faith that God is at work in their lives. End with a Glory Be, or a spontaneous prayer of thanksgiving to God for inspiring your volunteer to serve.

The Discernment Continues

By now this process should sound familiar. It is a continuation of the discernment process described earlier in the book. Discernment never ends. In every stage of life, we find time to stop and ask, "Where is God in all of this? Where is Christ calling me today?" By modeling it for relatively short moments in your parishioners' lives—simple decisions to assist with ministry in the parish—you are helping them build the habit for momentous life decisions as well. And who knows? A lot of Church moments surprise us and become significant life moments as well: vocations, lifetime friendships, and even soul-saving decisions made because of the Christ-like compassion we discovered in a parishioner.

We must practice discernment with all five levels of volunteers. It is just as important for the parish money counters, the social committee members, the prayer group, the pastor, the parish attorney, the Crop walk helper, the catechist, and the linen cleaner. The unexpected benefit of setting Level 1 and 2 volunteers free is that their amazement may draw them deeper:

"She wants me to prayerfully consider whether I will bake cookies for another year? She must really value my ministry. Maybe I can do more. Maybe I will prepare a dish for the homeless shelter."

Chapter 10

Jesus-Style Recruiting and the Reign of God

Forming Warm Bodies into Disciples is not only good for your program; it is part of building the Reign of God.

I have a confession to make.

Throughout my twenty years of parish and diocesan ministry, I made a private vow that I would never ask anyone to do something that I myself wasn't already doing or willing to do. As a diocesan employee, I would never call upon a parish leader to meet a diocesan standard without providing the practical tools that he or she needed to meet that standard. And I would never, NEVER, heap burdens on others.

I have broken all of those rules with the writing of this book. I fear that this book is very big on ideas, and not big enough on practical helps. Most of all, I know that this book proposes a lot of additional work for pastoral leaders. It will take an incredible amount of negotiation and sifting to level your ministries. You will need extensive resources to build your Warm Market. You could spend hours and hours organizing face-to-face recruitment campaigns. Your people will spend an almost unimaginable amount of time mentoring, discerning, sharing faith and finding ways to constructively praise your volunteers. Even if you managed to do all that, would you even *consider* setting all of your volunteers free every year? I wonder.

> **Jesus-Style Recruitment Tip #10: Get to work.**
>
> "As you go, proclaim the Good News, 'The kingdom of heaven has come near.'"
>
> Matthew 10:7

Have I proposed a ridiculously large amount of work? Have I heaped too great a burden on you?

Of course I have!

Despite all of that, I feel compelled not to issue an apology, but a challenge. In good faith, I accept the same challenge. It is neither original nor complicated. It applies to your work with volunteers, yes, but it extends even further, to the rest of your work, to your relationships, to your life. The challenge lies in the first word of the title: Jesus-Style. I set out to write a book about helpful hints to recruit parish volunteers, and I ended up writing a book about forming disciples. As I attempted to tie all of this back to the Gospel testimonies about Jesus, I was repeatedly drawn to Jesus's urgent proclamation that "the Kingdom of God has come near." (Mark 1:15). I felt more and more compelled to center this work around building the Reign of God.

Be Christ for others. Allow the Good News of Jesus to penetrate your life. Ask God to show you every day the people around you who most need that Good News. Pass the Word on; teach others to do the same. Help those in your care to become disciples.

We know this is what Jesus wants us to do. This is WHY we do what we do. So, what's stopping us? Let's get back to work!

Appendix

(Permission is given to reproduce all pages of the Appendix)

Jesus-Style Recruiting

WORKSHEET 1   LEVEL YOUR PARISH!

Jesus-Style Recruitment Tip#1: Meet people where they are. As Jesus was walking along, he saw a man called Matthew sitting at the tax booth; and he said to him, 'Follow me.' And he got up and followed him. Matthew 9:9

Directions: With your parish team, list as many ministries as you can for each of the levels below. Try to come up with enough ministries so that you can invite every member of your parish to do something.

Level 1 – Providers

These are people who do, make or prepare things for parish functions, often from the comfort of their homes. Time commitment is flexible and occasional, and attendance at parish events is optional. No training is required. *Examples: prayer intercessors, bakers of goods for program events, crafters, linen preparers, senders of greeting cards or emails, and donors of other goods.*

Level 2 - Helpers

This type of ministry is short-term and limited in scope. It requires little or no advance training, and minimal commitment beyond showing up. Recruits come right in off the street and go to work. *Examples: set up and cleanup crews, picnic helpers, greeters, office helpers, hall monitors, chaperones, car wash or fundraising volunteers.*

Level 3 – Professional Career Volunteers

These volunteers have been trained for work outside the parish, and can lend special skills to a parish event or ministry. Training required by a parish is minimal, but the time commitment varies with the task for which they are needed. *Examples: carpenters, professional cleaners, nurses, crafters, decorators, certified teachers, theologians, scientists, lawyers, engineers, architects.*

Level 4 - Semi-skilled Volunteers

This level of ministry requires orientation, some training and an occasional retreat or day of renewal. Volunteers may serve regularly, even weekly, but perform duties that do not require much preparation. *Examples: catechist aides, retreat chaperones, planning teams for key events.*

Level 5 – Skilled Volunteers

These volunteers perform their ministry regularly, often weekly or more frequently. They require not just orientation, but significant ongoing training and formation. They regularly prepare for their service. They may be groomed to head their ministry, or eventually even become a parish staff member.

Examples: catechists, pastoral musicians, liturgy coordinators, retreat leaders, parish social outreach minister.

Figure 1.

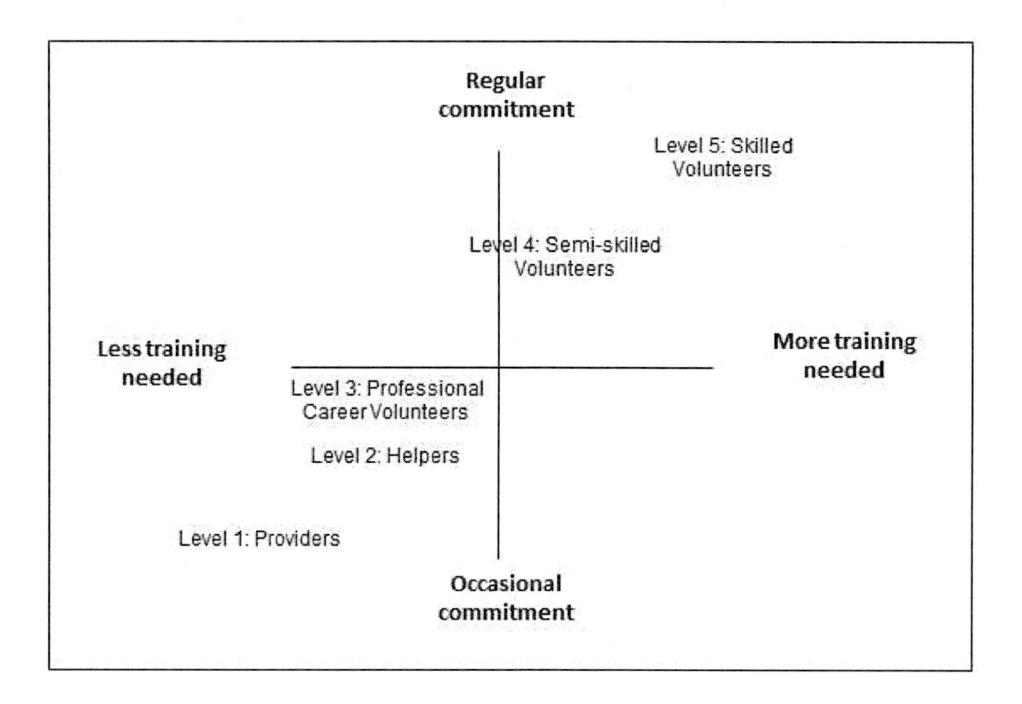

WORKSHEET 2   WARM MARKET COLD MARKET RECRUITING

Jesus-Style Recruitment Tip#2: Bring the Good News to Everyone "Go therefore and make disciples of all nations, baptizing them in the name of the Father and of the Son and of the Holy Spirit…" Matthew 28:19

COLD MARKET - Potential volunteers whom you don't know directly, parishioners with whom you have less contact.

Some Examples:

- Couples/Families that show up for sacraments after years away from the Church
- Registered parishioners who attend infrequently
- Inactive spouses of active members and extended family members of parishioners
- Public figures who are known to be Catholic but have no parish
- Registered parishioners who don't fully participate in the celebration of the Eucharist

How do we warm these people up?

WARM MARKET - Potential volunteers who are receptive to the idea of serving…or at least open to the person who is inviting them into ministry.

Directions: BRAINSTORM - Your list of 100 (okay, 30!) parishioners who are "warm" to you. Start with your closest friends and work outward.

HANDOUT 1   **RECRUITING, JESUS-STYLE**

Jesus-Style Recruitment Tip#3: Share the rewards of the Kingdom.

And he said to them, "Truly I tell you, there is no one who has left house or wife or brothers or parents or children, for the sake of the kingdom of God, who will not get back very much more in this age, and in the age to come eternal life." - Luke 18:29-30

1. An old-fashioned (i.e., as old as the Gospels) recruiting method

Step 1: Prioritize and select one ministry area for recruitment: evangelization, pastoral care, liturgy, catechesis, community building…etc. What is your area of greatest need or interest this year?

Step 2: Make sure that ministry area is multi-leveled (as identified in Worksheet 1).

Step 3: Parish Leader(s) Recruit Core Team

- Number Needed: 4 or 5 Core Team Members

- Qualities Needed: People already committed to the ministry area you have chosen. These could be pastoral council members or others who are already active in the ministry.

- Commitment required for Core Team: 1 month of recruiting, attendance at *Ministry Area Orientation 1 & 2* and occasional phone calls to recruiters.

- Recruiting Event: *Core Team Meeting*. Core team members learn about why, whom, and how to recruit.

Step 4: Core Team Invites Recruiters

- Number Needed: 8-10 Recruiters (Each Core Team member recruits at least 2)

- Qualities Needed: People with strong commitment to the parish and willing to learn about the ministry area. They do not necessarily need to be people who will DO the ministry.

- Commitment required for Recruiters: Attendance at *Ministry Area Orientation 1&2*, 1 month of recruiting, and making 1 or 2 calls to volunteers whom they have recruited.

- Recruiting Event: Personal meeting with Core Team Member.

Step 5: Recruiters find volunteers.

- Number needed: 16-20 Volunteers (Each recruiter finds 2).

- Qualities needed: People willing to learn about the ministry area.

- Commitment required for volunteers: Attendance at *Ministry Area Orientation 2*. Additional commitment will vary with the level of ministry they choose.

HANDOUT 2   STEP 3: Parish Leader(s) Recruit Core Team

MEETING: CORE TEAM MEETING

GOAL: Inspire Core Team to take part in recruiting process.

TAKES PLACE: Just before Month 1

LED BY: Parish Leader(s)

AUDIENCE: Core Team candidates

1. Prayer. Gospel reading from Mark 1:16-20, or another selection about the calling of the disciples.

2. Share what ignited your personal zeal for the Gospel. Ask your guests to talk about what has inspired their faith. Help them to see the power and joy that comes from passing on the faith, and to connect that joy to the ministry of _____. Don't rush over this step. Make sure that everyone is with you before you continue the process. Once you have established love for sharing faith as a given, turn to the concrete task that you would like them to do.

3. Invite them to be part of multiplying the ministry of the parish. Ask them to be your Core Team, recruiters of recruiters for the ministry of _____. Tell them that this phase of the process is simple, but not necessarily easy: you would like them to find two people to recruit volunteers. Be clear that in addition to recruiting recruiters, you want your Core Team to provide encouragement and support to their recruiters, and attend an orientation session for the ministry with their recruiters.

4. Share a list of ideal qualities for a volunteer recruiter.

5. Lead a mini-brainstorming session of possible recruiters, using a master list of current or inactive volunteers. Who knows? You may surface enough names here to jump right into the work!

6. Give them an outline of a process to use when recruiting recruiters.

7. Deadlines: 1) a deadline, in one month's time, when they should turn in the names of their two recruits to you and 2) a check-in time, two weeks down the road, when they will report on their progress.

8. Open invitation: Are they willing to take on this challenge?

METHOD: PROCESS FOR CORE TEAM MEMBERS TO RECRUIT RECRUITERS

RECRUITING TAKES PLACE: Month 1

GOAL: 2 Recruiters

1. Brainstorm. With a spouse or close friend from the parish, make a list of people who might be good recruiters. Do you know anyone who has shown an ability to reach out to others? This person need not be an extrovert; many strong introverts are comfortable relating one-to-one with people. There are a growing number of people who own their own home-based business. They are accustomed to inviting people to join them – this task could be a natural fit.

2. Verify. Pass your initial list by your leader. He/She can verify whether another member of the Core Team is recruiting people on your list already. Your leader might also be aware of why it would be particularly appropriate – or inappropriate – to issue the invitation now.

3. Schedule. Set up a time to meet the potential volunteer. It would be best to make this invitation in person, say, after a Sunday Mass, but a phone call may be the only workable way to get through to them. Request some time to talk in person, either at one of your houses, at church, or even at a favorite coffee shop. If pressed, tell the truth: you would like him/her to help you with an important church ministry, but would prefer to talk about it in person when you are both free of interruptions and distractions. If pressed further about the ministry, tell him/her that you think he/she is ideally suited to help grow the parish's ministry of _____ as a volunteer recruiter. However, do not let him/her give an immediate yes or no on the phone. Explain that you would like to explain the terms of the ministry fully in person.

4. Meet. Set up a private meeting with each of your potential recruiters. When you get together, start by sharing your own version of what sets your faith on fire, and why the ministry of catechesis is important to you. Tell them why you agreed to be a member of the Core Team, recruiting recruiters. Explain that just as your role is fixed for a set duration, you are inviting them to a role with a distinct beginning and end. You are asking them to be a recruiter of two volunteers.

To help them get a sense of the process, share the list of responsibilities of a volunteer recruiter and a list of the ministries for which they would be recruiting. Ask them if anyone comes to mind immediately as they look at these qualities. Then offer any other ideas that you have found helpful for recruiting. Finally, give them two dates: 1) a *Ministry Area Orientation* session for volunteer recruiters with the Core Team; and 2) a deadline when they should turn in names of people who have accepted their initial invitation to explore the ministry of catechesis.

5. Invite. Conclude your meeting with the same open invitation that you received when you were recruited. Are they willing to take on this special assignment? If they need time to discern, set a time when you can call them to discuss it. You can also invite them to postpone their decision until after they have attended *Ministry Area Orientation 1*.

HANDOUT 3   **STEP 4: Core Team Recruits Recruiters**

MEETING: MINISTRY ORIENTATION 1

GOAL: Help recruiters catch the vision of the ministry for which they are recruiting

TAKES PLACE: Before end of Month 1

LED BY: Coordinators of Ministry Area, Parish Leader(s)

AUDIENCE: Recruiters, Core Team

Meeting elements:

1. Prayer. If possible, use a Scripture reading showing biblical roots of the ministry for which you are recruiting. Incorporate a formal reading of the Parish Mission Statement into this prayer as well. Invite participants to reflect on how the Scripture passage and the Mission Statement are connected.

2. Lead faith sharing on the passage, with emphasis upon questions like, How do you think Christ is calling you to spread the Good News to others? Where or when have you sensed Christ's presence most strongly?

3. Personal faith witnesses from participants in the ministry. Volunteers share what being part of the ministry has done for them, how they have benefited from participating, and how doing this ministry has challenged or nurtured their faith.

4. Presentation on levels of ministry within this area.

5. Q & A session between recruiters and ministry volunteers.

6. Instructions on how to recruit volunteers from parish leader(s).

METHOD: PROCESS FOR RECRUITING VOLUNTEERS

RECRUITING TAKES PLACE: Month 2

GOAL: 2 potential volunteers to attend the *Ministry Area Orientation*

Volunteer Recruiters can follow a method similar to the one used by the Core Team in recruiting them.

1. Brainstorm. With a spouse or close friend from the parish, make a list of people who might be good volunteers in the ministry area. Do you know people who might simply enjoy learning about this are of church ministry? Think of the enrichment of learning more about this aspect of Catholic life as a primary benefit of volunteering, and invite volunteers with this awesome benefit in mind. Think outside of the box – see where this idea of learning more about faith leads you.

2. Verify. Pass your initial list by your parish leader. He/She can verify whether another volunteer recruiter has already enlisted anyone on your list. Your parish leader might also be aware of why it would be particularly appropriate – or inappropriate – to issue the invitation now.

3. Schedule. Set up a time to meet the potential volunteer. Tell them up front that you think they might enjoy growing in their faith through the ministry of _____. Request time to talk in person, either at one of your houses, at church, or even at a favorite coffee shop. Follow the same rules that we listed in other steps of this process: stress that you would like their undivided attention by meeting face-to-face.

4. Meet. Set up a private meeting with each of your potential volunteers. When you get together, start by sharing why you are recruiting for this ministry, and why it is important to you. If you have served in the ministry directly, tell them why it was such a good experience for you. Explain that just as your role of recruiting is fixed for a set duration, you are inviting them to a role with a distinct beginning and end – a one year term.

To help them get a sense of the process, give them the leveled list of volunteer opportunities for the ministry. Reassure them that there is a level of involvement for just about every time frame. Finally give them the date of *Ministry Area Orientation 2,* where they will hear a lot more specifics about the ministry.

5. Invite. Ask the potential volunteer if they would consider volunteering for this area of ministry. Would he/she be willing to attend the *Ministry Area Orientation 2* to learn more?

Jesus-Style Recruiting

HANDOUT 4 STEP 5: Recruiters find Volunteers

MEETING: MINISTRY AREA ORIENTATION 2

This is just a functional title. Give your event a nicer name!

GOAL: Inspire potential volunteers to take part in the ministry

TAKES PLACE: End of Month 2

LED BY: Coordinators of Ministry Area, Parish Leader(s)

AUDIENCE: Potential Volunteers, Recruiters, Core Team

Meeting elements:

1. Gathering: Recruiters greet volunteers whom they recruited, and sit with them.

2. Prayer. If possible, use a Scripture reading showing biblical roots of the ministry for which you are recruiting. Incorporate a formal reading of the Parish Mission Statement into this prayer as well. Invite participants to reflect on how the Scripture passage and the Mission Statement are connected.

3. Lead faith sharing on the passage, with emphasis upon questions like, How do you think Christ is calling you to spread the Good News to others? Where or when have you sensed Christ's presence most strongly?

4. Personal faith witnesses from participants in the ministry. Volunteers share what being part of the ministry has done for them, how they have benefited from participating, and how doing this ministry has challenged or nurtured their faith.

5. Presentation on levels of ministry within this area, and requirements for training, if applicable.

6. Q & A session between potential volunteers and ministry volunteers.

7. Prayer and Challenge led by Parish Leaders(s): Have you heard something that touched you? Do you sense God's call to participate in this ministry? Parish leader(s) and coordinators of ministry area encourage all to pray for and promote the ministry, and consider volunteer. Presenters stay around after meeting for questions.

8. If potential volunteers do not give definite answer to the challenge at the meeting, recruiters follow up with a phone call one week later.

VOLUNTEER OBSERVATION FORM

Date of Observation: _____ Time: _____

Volunteer Name: _____ Observer: _____

Ministry: _____

NOTES

Something I noticed that you did particularly well:

_____

_____

_____

One way that you witnessed to the Gospel of Jesus was:

_____

_____

_____

One area where you could improve or grow in your ministry is:

_____

_____

_____

For further study or skill development, I suggest this resource:

_____

_____

_____

Additional Comments:

_____

_____

Thank you for your continued dedication to ministry!

_____   _____

Signature of ministry leader   Date

EXAMPLE

Fr. Keith Boisvert's letter to
parish ministry leaders

28 December 2010

Dear (First Name),

It has become our tradition now to gather all of our ministry leaders for dinner as a way of beginning the New Year and acknowledging those who are retiring from positions of leadership. Our pastoral staff is once again busy planning the menu and will be present to serve you in McElroy Hall during our seventh annual Ministry Leaders Dinner on Saturday 5 February 2011 at 6:30 PM—and we hope you will join us!

This is our small way of saying "thank you" for collaborating together with us in ministry. Your dedicated efforts as a ministry leader help the life of Saint Katharine Drexel faith community to run smoothly. Your service as a ministry coordinator also helps our many volunteers to feel connected as contributors to our stated mission of *"realizing the Kingdom of God"*.

I would like to invite you to reaffirm your intention to continue coordinating your ministry during 2011. Each year, through this invitation, you have the opportunity to express your desire about continuing in your role. This annual dinner will give us an opportunity to express our appreciation to anyone who chooses to retire as a coordinator for one reason or another—and so we hope you will join us even if you are planning to leave your role as ministry coordinator.

Please prayerfully consider if you are willing to continue serving in your present leadership role during calendar year 2011, and complete the enclosed form indicating your intention. Please also indicate whether or not you will be able to join us for dinner at 6:30 PM on Saturday 5 February and if you will be bringing a guest. I look forward to seeing you there!

Sincerely,

(Rev.) Keith W. Boisvert

Pastor

EXAMPLE

**Fr. Keith Boisvert's letter to
parish ministry leaders**

RESPONSE FORM

SEVENTH ANNUAL MINISTRY LEADERS DINNER

McELROY HALL

5 FEBRUARY 2011 @ 6:30 PM

Name: _____ Phone: _____

Ministry: _____

_____ I would like to continue coordinating this ministry during 2011.

_____ I would like to retire from coordinating this ministry, and

    (1) _____ would like assistance in arranging another coordinator; or

    (2) _____ recommend the following person to be considered as my successor:

    _____

_____ I will attend the Seventh Annual Ministry Leaders Dinner on 5 February 2011.

_____ I will bring the following guest: _____

_____ I have the following dietary needs: